COMPREHENSiON

Geoff Barton

Oxford University Press

Oxford University Press, Great Clarendon Street, Oxford OX2 6DP

Oxford New York
Athens Auckland Bangkok Bogota Bombay
Buenos Aires Calcutta Cape Town Dar es Salaam
Delhi Florence Hong Kong Istanbul Karachi
Kuala Lumpur Madras Madrid Melbourne
Mexico City Nairobi Paris Singapore
Taipei Tokyo Toronto Warsaw

and associated companies in
Berlin Ibadan

Oxford is a trade mark of Oxford University Press

First published 1997
Reprinted 1997, 1998

ISBN 0 19 831300 4

Designed by Ian Foulis and Associates, Saltash, Cornwall.

Printed in Spain

Contents

Section 3 POETRY

Section 4 NON-FICTION

Comprehension to 14

Introduction to the Teacher

Defining Comprehension

Comprehension to 14 has a fairly self-explanatory title. But by 'comprehension' we mean something more than the weekly fact-quacking tests many of us recall from pre-GCSE days. It isn't a book of dusty snippets from worthy autobiographies and faded fiction. I hope foremost that it's a collection of lively and stimulating reading resources – interesting in their own right. That was the starting-point for the book: can we collect texts which students will enjoy reading? Reading pleasure is essential to close reading. If you don't find any interest in the text, you won't want to read on, let alone analyse your response.

That's not to say that every text will appeal to every reader. But I have tried to select a variety of unexpected resources – the kinds of texts which we don't normally associate with 'comprehension' – as well as marshalling some of the familiar big guns of the National Curriculum.

Comprehension is a bit of a deadly word. Its association for many of us is with dullness, passivity, and a mechanical approach to learning English – hence, in recent years, the increased emphasis on active reading and the more fashionable term 'reading and response'.

But for all its liveliness, the response approach to reading has been problematic. Whilst it rightly places greater emphasis on legitimizing students' feelings about a piece of writing – encouraging them to say what they think about it – it has, in many of its manifestations, paid too little attention to close reading, as if there were something authoritarian, prescriptive, or divisive about wanting students to read accurately for detail. Many of us, locked in lengthy exam invigilation sessions, have pondered GCSE English papers – particularly those testing reading skills – and worried about the paucity of direct questions about understanding the text.

Certainly the reviewers who responded to the early drafts of *Comprehension to 14* (all of them classroom teachers) felt that more straightforward factual questions, designed to test knowledge of the text, were an important addition. Questions of this type have been duly increased. Perversely, such questions are not the ones which alienate or deter less confident readers. They in fact give students reassurance, a sense of security that they're following what's going on, before being coaxed into the deeper waters of response and evaluation.

Comprehension to 14 is designed, in other words, to develop and assess reading skills at a variety of levels. But it is based on the assumption that you cannot progress sensitively and wisely into a text unless you clearly understand what it is about. The organizational features of the book therefore reflect this approach.

Organization

The book is divided into the major forms of the reading curriculum – that is, Fiction, Drama, Poetry, and Non-Fiction. The texts have been chosen to cover the ability range of Levels 3 to 8 at Key Stage 3 – but the bulk of texts are designed to be used with your average students, those working around Levels 4, 5, and 6. Texts are organized by genre, to encourage students to gain a deeper sense of the conventions and language features of different forms of writing.

Within the Drama and Poetry sections, texts are grouped according to a perception of their accessibility – easier texts begin the section, more demanding ones come later.

The Fiction and Non-Fiction sections are organized on a slightly different principle: although the sections as a whole are not organized in terms of difficulty, where two or more examples of each genre are included, the more accessible text comes first. So, for example, under 'Ghost Stories', the extract from Robert Westall's *Rosalie* comes before the more challenging Franz Kafka story, *The Knock at the Manor Gate*.

On the page, we have designed the book to give students reassurance. It isn't a book of comprehension tests. It is designed instead to build students' confidence as they develop their own reading skills. Hence the following features:

Illustrations to provide an imaginative context for each text and to draw students into the subject-matter.

'Before reading' prompts: these are questions to narrow the range of possibilities: the intention here is that students should gain a sense of what the text is likely to be like before they embark upon it. This should encourage more active reading. You may decide that students should discuss these prompts in pairs or small groups, or reflect upon them individually.

Word banks: the glossaries have been written to lower the reading level of all texts by giving students greater linguistic access to them. The words are arranged in alphabetical order. The priority has been functional glossing – that is, choosing definitions which work in this context to keep students reading.

'After reading' questions: these have been subdivided into A and B groupings. 'A' questions are the more direct, factual questions. They rely on students re-reading the text to find specific information about characters, themes, or topics. These are questions that provide support for less confident readers and usually serve as scaffolding for the later, more analytical questions. 'B' questions place greater emphasis upon analysis, response to language, judgements about wider issues in the text, and personal response.

I leave it to you to decide whether your students need to work through all of the questions, or a selection of them. Chances are your decision about using all or some of the questions will vary from one group to the next, according to your teaching aims and your students' reading skills. *Comprehension to 14* is intended as a flexible resource, and I hope that you find the organizational feature of A- and B-type questions helpful.

Extended assignments: these are designed to move students on from the texts. They almost always build upon knowledge of issues or language gained in the reading process, but then develop it. The first of the tasks is designed to be more accessible than those that follow. You might choose to give students choice over which assignment they work on; or you might be more prescriptive. That is up to you: the structure of the assignments is designed to enhance the possibilities for differentiation.

Conclusion

As you will see, *Comprehension to 14* is intended as much more than an off-the-shelf book of comprehension exercises. It has been written to re-emphasize the importance of understanding what has been read, to provide a range of new resources which match the requirements of the new curriculum, and to develop reading skills in students of all abilities at Key Stage 3.

In an age of such exciting developments in the textual demands placed upon young people, their capacity to respond quickly, accurately, and sensitively to texts of all kinds becomes even more important. I hope that *Comprehension to 14* helps them to become better readers.

Geoff Barton,
York

FICTION

Reading and responding to fiction

This section contains a range of fiction texts, including:
- stories from this century and from the past
- stories from a variety of cultures (for example, Czechoslovakia, the Caribbean, the USA, Britain)
- extracts as well as whole texts
- some stories, or extracts from stories, collected together to show different genres or categories of writing.

One of the ways in which human beings differ from all other animals is our love of stories. We tell stories to each other (jokes, gossip, soap opera plots, instructions). We watch them on screens (programmes, films, computer games). We read them in books, newspapers, and magazines (articles, novels, short stories, romance, photo stories, biographies ... and so on).

This section helps you to explore the way *fictional* stories – stories of the imagination – work in novels and short stories. It is designed to improve your skills in responding to fiction.

Key skills

- Following what happens in a story.
- Looking at the way different stories are structured.
- Looking at features like characterization and setting.
- Examining different writers' styles.
- Learning more about genres (categories of stories).

Berlie Doherty: Bella's Den

Advice panel: responding to fiction

As you read fiction, look out for:

- what the characters are like – their appearance, their behaviour, how they speak, what they think of each other, etc. Do you like them? Why?
- where the text is set: how does the writer make the place come to life – with strong atmosphere, lots of description, or just key details to make it feel real?
- how much the storyline holds your interest – is there suspense or tension as we try to work out what will happen next? Is the story straightforward, or does it jump from one plot to another to keep us in suspense?

Focus on setting

This extract from a short story gives a vivid description of a place that becomes important to the main character. By showing us the setting in so much detail, the writer is also able to tell us more about the characters, because we see the place through their eyes and learn about their reactions to where they are.

Before reading

As children we often like to make dares. This extract from a short story by Berlie Doherty revolves around such a dare. The narrator and her friend Bella have persuaded their parents to let them sleep out in the garden overnight. The noise of the owls sounds like 'people with really bad colds sneezing their heads off'. As a result the girls cannot sleep.

While they are lying awake, Bella issues her dare – to go into the woods and stay overnight in the den she has built beneath an old tree. Bella is confident and determined. She sets off straight away. The narrator has to think about it a little longer. She is not so sure about being farther away from the house all night. Then she decides: 'If Bella could do it, so could I'.

How do you feel about sleeping outdoors at night? Would you enjoy listening to nature all around, or would it terrify you?

Bella's Den

Word bank
vixen – female fox

I draped my sleeping-bag round my shoulders like a cloak, stuck my bare feet in my wellies and grabbed the packet of ginger nuts. By this time Bella was out of sight. The horses were in the garage and it would have made too much noise to get them out, so I flolopped through the farmyard after her till I'd worked my feet properly into the wellies, ran over the bridge and up the lane and searched in the moonlight for the muddy patch. I heard my sleeping-bag rip a bit on the barbed wire and reminded myself to look for any torn bits on the fence next day. It would never do for us to leave tracks behind us. Then I lost my footing and slid all the way down the bank. I'm proud to say I didn't yell out. My sleeping-bag finally fell off when I was crossing the river, and I stung myself on some nettles as I was trying to rescue it. But it was all worth it, every bit of agony was worth it, because of what happened next.

We must have been in the den for nearly an hour. There wasn't room for us both to lie down so we were sitting crouched together with Bella's sleeping-bag pulled across us both. We were both staring out into the night. It was so dark then that it didn't seem to have any depth. It was like a black curtain, just too far away to reach out and touch. Then the moon slid away from the clouds and through the trailing leaves covering the den it was suddenly as clear as day. And I think I was the first to see it. I was looking at the big mound below the den, and thinking how the moonlight made it look like a theatre with the stage lights on, and how deep and black those holes were, when I caught sight of a movement. I touched Bella's arm and she let out a little breath of, yes, she'd seen it too.

It was a fox. He seemed to grow out of the darkness of the hole, and then took shape as the moon lit him. He stood as if he had been turned to stone, and he was staring right at our den, right through the leaf strands, right at me. He was locked right in to me, reading the thoughts in my mind, and I daren't move or breathe, I daren't do anything but stare back at him, till my eyes were blurring. I thought I would pass out with holding myself so still, and my skin was ice-cold, frozen cold with fear.

Then all of a sudden he seemed to relax. He turned his head slightly, and as if it was a signal of some sort out came another, and another, four more shapes looming out of the hole, each one faster than the one before, bouncing out like infants in a school playground, tumbling red and brown and silvery white. The dog fox slunk off into the shadows. The other biggish fox, his vixen, sat just where he had been, just at the mouth of the hole, her ears pricked up and her head turning from time to time as she listened out for all kinds of sounds in the hills. But the three cubs had come out to play. They cuffed each other and fell over and rolled about, jumped on each other, jumped on her, hid from each other and roly-polyed right down to the river. I could hear them breathing, and scuffling with their paws, I could hear the little puffs of sound they made when they biffed each other. It felt as if it

was the middle of the world, this little patch of ground where the foxes were playing, as if nothing else that was happening anywhere was as important as this.

I've no idea what the signal was, but the vixen suddenly turned her head, sharp. The cubs scrambled up the bank and one by one slid back inside it. She waited a moment, lifted her head slightly then just melted down into the hole after them, sliding like water into it. It went dark again, as if the moon had been put out. I strained my eyes and I'm not sure whether I really saw it or not, but there seemed to be another shape, like a dark fluttering where the hole was, and a dull white glow like the tip of a tail disappearing into it.

Funny, we didn't talk about the foxes the next day, Bella and I. I think we didn't need to.

Berlie Doherty

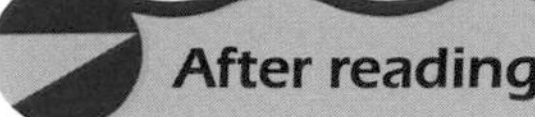

A

1 What is the den like? Which *one* of these words and phrases does not accurately describe it?
- **a** difficult to get to
- **b** cramped
- **c** dark
- **d** covered in leaves
- **e** smelly
- **f** has a big mound below it

2 How can you tell that the narrator is less confident in the countryside, as she makes her way to the den?

3 How can you tell that the narrator enjoys watching the fox cubs playing?

4 Which one of these words best describes Bella at the start of the story? Write a sentence to explain your choice.

confident loner independent determined rude

5 Which one of these words or phrases best sums up the narrator?

nervous uncertain keen to go along less confident confused

B

6 'Funny, we didn't talk about the foxes the next day, Bella and I. I think we didn't need to.' Say in your own words what you think this might mean.

7 We never learn the narrator's name. Do you think this matters? As you read the extract, did it make you feel less involved in the story, or didn't it matter? Try to explain your response.

8 At the start of the extract it is Bella's den. By the end the narrator goes there alone, keeping it secret. How has the narrator changed by the end of the story?

Extended assignments

1 Imagine you are the narrator in this story (we never learn her name). When you get back home you are still thinking about what you saw. Write your diary for that memorable night. You should mention:

- how you felt when Bella said she was going to the den
- your first impressions of what the den was like
- how you felt as you watched the foxes
- how you felt by the end of the night
- why the den is now so important to you

2 Choose one of the following topics to write about:

a a time when you accepted a dare

b a time when you have been fascinated by something in nature

c a time when you slept out overnight – in a tent or under the stars

To make your writing lively and interesting, try to describe what you remember in detail (sounds, smells, sights). Describe your feelings. Try to give the reader a vivid impression of what it was like to be you on that day.

James Berry: The Banana Tree

Focus on atmosphere This extract from a short story by James Berry describes a hurricane. It shows us how powerful writing can make us feel new experiences and sensations.

Before reading

We all know what storms can be like, but have you ever experienced a hurricane? James Berry, writing about such a storm in Jamaica, uses language to make us feel that we are there.

His main character, Gustus, comes from a poor family. He has been tending a banana tree, planning to sell the fruit to buy shoes, so that he can go on a school cricket-team outing. When the hurricane approaches, Gustus's family goes to a shelter – but Gustus is determined to get back home, to protect the banana tree from the storm.

Would you take a risk like this in order to get something you really wanted?

Word bank

accumulation – build-up
beyond recognition – so that he no longer knew it
breadfruit – a tree of the Pacific islands with seedless fruit
debris – waste
dismay – worry
festered – unclean
gully – ditch
limb – branch
molested – harmed
nable string – 'navel string', umbilical cord. When Gustus was born, the banana tree was planted for him in a traditional ceremony, and his umbilical cord was planted under it
paralysed – stopped him from moving
torso – body

The Banana Tree

When his eyes opened, his round face was turned up to a festered sky. Above the tormented trees a zinc sheet writhed, twisted and somersaulted in the tempestuous flurry. Leaves of all shapes and sizes were whirling and diving like attackers around the zinc sheet. As Gustus turned to get up, a bullet-drop of rain struck his temple. He shook his head, held grimly to the tree trunk and struggled to his feet.

Where the road was clear, he edged along the bank. Once, when the wind staggered him, he recovered with his legs wide apart. Angrily, he stretched out his hands with clenched fists and shouted: 'I almos' hol' you dat time ... come solid like dat again an' we fight like man an' man!'

When Gustus approached the river he had to cross, it was flooded and blocked beyond recognition. Pressing his chest against the gritty road-bank the boy closed his weary eyes on the brink of the spating river. The wrecked footbridge had become the harbouring fort for all the debris, branches and monstrous tree-trunks which the river swept along its course. The river was still swelling. More accumulation arrived each moment, ramming and pressing the bridge. Under pressure it was cracking and shifting minutely towards a turbulent forty-foot fall.

Gustus had seen it! A feeling of dismay paralysed him, reminding him of his foolish venture. He scraped his cheek on the bank looking back. But how can he go back. He has no strength to go back. His house is nearer than the school. An' Pappy will only strap him for nothin'... for nothin'... no shoes, nothin' when the hurricane is gone.

With trembling fingers he tied up the remnants of his shirt. He made a bold step and the wind half-lifted him, ducking him in the muddy flood. He sank to his neck. Floating leaves, sticks, coconut husks, dead ratbats, and all manner of feathered creatures and refuse surrounded him. Forest vines under the water entangled him. But he struggled desperately until he clung to the laden bridge, and climbed up among leafless branches.

His legs were bruised and bore deep scratches, but steadily he moved up on the slimy pile. He felt like a man at sea, in the heart of a storm, going up the mast of a ship. He rested his feet on a smooth log that stuck to the water-splashed heap like a black torso. As he strained up for another grip the torso came to life and leaped from under his feet. Swiftly sliding down, he grimly clutched some brambles.

The urgency of getting across became more frightening, and he gritted his teeth and dug his toes into the debris, climbing with maddened determination. But a hard gust of wind slammed the wreck, pinning him like a motionless lizard. For a minute the boy was stuck there, panting, swelling his naked ribs.

He stirred again and reached the top. He was sliding over a breadfruit limb when a flutter startled him. As he looked and saw the clean-head crow and glassy-eyed owl close together, there was a powerful jolt. Gustus flung himself into the air and fell in the expanding water on the other side. When he surfaced, the river had dumped the entire wreckage into the gurgling gully. For once the wind helped. It blew him to land.

Gustus was in a daze when he reached his house. Mud and rotten leaves covered his head and face, and blood caked around a gash on his chin. He bent down, shielding himself behind a tree-stump whose white heart was a needly splinter; murdered by the wind.

He could hardly recognize his yard. The terrorized trees that stood writhing in turmoil. Their thatched house had collapsed like an open umbrella that was given a heavy blow. He looked the other way and whispered, 'Is still dere! Dat's a miracle... Dat's a miracle.'

Dodging the wind, he staggered from tree to tree until he got to his own tormented banana tree. Gustus hugged the tree. 'My nable string!' he cried. 'My nable string! I know you would stan'

up to it, I know you would.'

The bones of the tree's stalky leaves were broken, and the wind lifted them and harrassed them. And over Gustus's head the heavy fruit swayed and swayed. The props held the tree, but they were squeaking and slipping. And around the plant the roots stretched and trembled, gradually surfacing under loose earth.

With the rags of his wet shirt flying off his back, Gustus was down busily on his knees, bracing, pushing, tightening the props. One by one he was adjusting them until a heavy rush of wind knocked him to the ground. A prop fell on him, but he scrambled to his feet and looked up at the thirteen-hand bunch of bananas. 'My good tree,' he bawled, 'hol' yo' fruit... keep it to yo' heart like a mudder savin' her baby! Dohn let the wicked wind t'row you to the groun'... even if it t'row me to the groun'. I will not leave you.'

But several attempts to replace the prop were futile. The force of the wind against his weight was too much for him. He thought of a rope to lash the tree to anything, but it was difficult to make his way to the kitchen, which, separate from the house, was still standing. The invisible hand of the wind tugged, pushed and forcefully restrained him. He got down and crawled on his belly into the earth-floor kitchen. As he showed himself with the rope, the wind tossed him, like washing on the line, against his tree.

The boy was hurt! He looked crucified against the tree. The spike of the wind was slightly withdrawn. He fell, folded on the ground. He lay there unconscious. And the wind had no mercy for him. It shoved him, poked him, and molested his clothes like muddy newspaper against the tree.

As darkness began to move in rapidly, the wind grew more vicious and surged a mighty gust which struck the resisting kitchen. It was heaved to the ground in a rubbled pile. The brave wooden hut had been shielding the banana tree but in its death-fall missed it by inches. The wind charged again and the soft tree gurgled – the fruit was torn from it and plunged to the ground.

James Berry

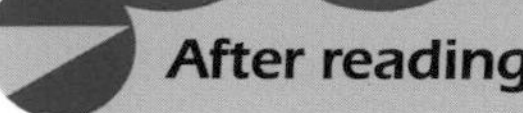

After reading

A

1 In the first paragraph, James Berry writes about 'a bullet-drop' of rain. What does this make you think the rain is like?

2 Look at the second paragraph. How does Gustus react to the powerful wind?

3 Find a sentence in the extract which you think best shows the power of the hurricane.

4 Is the wind totally against Gustus, or does it also seem at times to be on his side?

5 When Gustus says 'Dat's a miracle', what is he referring to?

B

6 Look at these descriptions of the wind:
'The invisible hand of the wind tugged ...'
'...the wind had no mercy for him ...'
'It shoved him, poked him, and molested his clothes ...'
What picture of the wind do these images create?

7 What impression do you get of Gustus from the extract?

8 Look more closely at the first paragraph. How does James Berry create a powerful impression of the hurricane?

Extended assignments

1 What would the story look like as a film sequence? Create a storyboard to show how the story develops. Start with the first bullet-drop of rain, and then show the rest of the story. How would you show the power of the storm and the strong sense of atmosphere?
Remember that the quality of your drawings is not the most important part of this task. You need to show how you would create atmosphere and tell the story of Gustus in the hurricane. Use labels and speech bubbles to make your ideas clearer, if you wish.
Aim to use 12 to 16 frames to tell the story.

2 Write your own strongly atmospheric description of being caught in bad weather – for example, fog, thick snow, driving rain. Like James Berry, use language to show the powerful force of nature against human beings.

Rosa Guy: She

Focus on characterization

This extract uses one of the most important techniques in fiction and drama. It brings together characters who don't like each other and shows us how they behave.

Before reading

Rosa Guy's short story uses different techniques to show us what the characters are like. It describes what they look like, shows us what they think of each other, presents the way they speak. It is also told through the eyes of one character – a powerful way of showing us the thoughts of a main character.

Some people find that they don't enjoy a story if they don't like the main character. Which main character from a story you have read did you most like? Why?

She

Word bank
grievances – complaints
linoleum – floor-covering
mules – casual shoes
necessity – something that must be done

'Just where do you think you're going?' she said.

'To the bathroom,' I said.

'No, you're not,' she said. 'Not before you wash up these dishes.'

'This is a matter of urgent necessity,' I said. I hated that even my going to the bathroom had to be questioned.

'Don't want to hear,' she said. 'I'm sick and tired of emergency, emergency every night after dinner. Get to that sink.'

'I'll wash the dishes,' Linda said. She got up and started to clear off the table. I slipped out of the kitchen. The angry voice followed me down the hall:

'Linda, don't keep letting your sister get away with everything.'

'I don't mind – really, Dorine,' Linda said.

'That girl's just too damn lazy...' I shut the bathroom door to muffle the sounds of her grievances against me. She didn't like me. She never had. And I didn't care. Stepmothers...!

Searching the bottom of the hamper for the science fiction magazine I had hidden beneath the dirty clothes, I sat on the toilet and began to read to get out of this world – as far from her as I could get.

From the day she walked into our house she'd been on to me. I was lying on my bed reading when she and Daddy pushed into my room without knocking. Our eyes locked. She didn't speak. Neither did I.

I was in a panic. Daddy had forbidden me to read fairy tales. 'At twelve years old! You too old,' he'd said. He wanted me to read only school books. I hadn't had time to hide the book of fairy tales beneath my mattress as I usually did. I curled up around it, praying to keep his eyes from it.

But Daddy was only showing her the apartment. So she had to turn to inspect my almost bare room. When she looked back at me, her eyes said: What are you doing reading in this miserable room instead of doing something useful around this terrible house? My eyes answered: What's it to you?

They left the room the way they'd come. Abruptly. Hearing their footsteps going towards the kitchen, I got up and followed. Linda was in the kitchen, washing fish for our dinner. When they went in, Linda looked up and smiled.

'What a lovely girl,' Dorine said, and the shock of her American accent went through me. What was Daddy doing with an American woman! 'She's got to be the prettiest child I ever did see. My name is Dorine,' she said.

From the first she had chosen Linda over me. Maybe because Linda was pretty, with her long, thick hair and clear brown eyes and brown velvet skin. I was plain-looking. Or maybe because Linda was two years older – already a teenager.

'You're Daddy's friend,' Linda said, batting her long black eyelashes the way she always did whenever someone paid her a compliment. 'I didn't know Daddy had a lady friend.' Daddy gave Linda a quick look and she changed to: 'My name is Linda. And that's' – she pointed to where I stood in the doorway – 'the baby. Her name is Gogi.'

But Dorine had already turned away from Linda to inspect the kitchen. And suddenly I saw our kitchen and the sweat of embarrassment almost drowned me: the sink was leaking and had a pan under it to catch the dirty water; the windowpanes were broken and stuffed with newspapers to keep out winter; the linoleum was worn, showing the soft wood beneath.

And she wore furs. Our mother had never worn furs. Not even when Daddy had had lots of money. People from the tropics didn't think of wearing things like furs. And the way Dorine looked around – nose squinched up, mouth pulled back – judging us, West Indians.

Daddy stood in the middle of the kitchen, quieter than usual – big, broad, handsome in his black overcoat, around his arm the black crepe band of mourning. His hands were deep in the pockets of his grey wool suit. And she hit out at him: 'Damn, Harry, how can you live like this!'

Linda stopped smiling then. Daddy's eyebrows quivered. My mouth got tight with satisfaction. Daddy had a mean temper. I waited for him to blast her out of our house and out of our lives. She had socked us where we hurt – our pride.

'How you mean?' Daddy had said. 'We ain't live so. You see mi restaurant…' So, he had known her while our mother was still alive '…I lose it,' he said. 'Mi wife dead. I sell mi house, mi furniture, mi car. I – I – mi friend let me stay here for a time – but it only for a short time.' He was begging! I hated that he stood there begging.

'If it's only one minute, that's one minute too damn long,' she had said.

Lifting my head from the science fiction magazine to turn a page, I heard the sound of pots banging against pans in the kitchen. And I heard Dorine's footsteps in the hall. I waited for the knob to turn on the bathroom door. She sometimes did that. But this time she went on into the living room. A short time later I heard the television playing.

It had been two years since the pointing, the ordering, the arranging and rearranging of our lives had begun. She had forced us to leave our old free apartment and move into her big one with its big rooms, its big kitchen and all those dozens of pots and pans for all things and all occasions. We had to listen to her constant: 'Cleanliness is next to godliness', and 'A good housekeeper has a place for everything and keeps everything in its place'. Like who told her that what we wanted most in life was to be housekeepers? I didn't!

Daddy let her get away with everything. He stayed out most days looking for work. And he spent evenings gambling with his friends. The times he spent at home he spent with her – laughing and joking in their bedroom. She entertained him to keep him there. I'd see her flashing around the house in her peach-coloured

satin dressing gown, her feet pushed into peach-coloured frilly mules, her big white teeth showing all across her face, her gown falling away to expose plump brown knees. Guess that's what he liked – that combination of peach satin and smooth brown skin.

She worked, a singer. Sometimes for weeks she'd be out on the road. The she'd come home with her friends and they'd do all that loud American talking and laughing. She sometimes brought us lovely things back from 'the road'. Blouses, underwear, coats. She won Linda's affection like that and might have won mine if I hadn't heard a man friend say to her one day: 'Dorine, it's bad enough you got yourself hooked up with that West Indian. But how did you manage to get in a family way?'

'Big Red,' she called him. 'I'm in love.'

'With all of 'em?' he asked.

'They come with the deal,' she said.

'Some deal,' he answered.

'You need to worry none, Big Red,' she said. 'They earn their keep.'

She saw me standing in the doorway then, and her big eyes stretched out almost to where I stood. Guilty. Her mouth opened. I walked away. I had heard enough. I went right in and told Linda. 'That's what she wants us around for,' I said. 'To be her maids.'

'Gogi,' Linda said. 'She probably didn't mean it that way at all.'

'What other way could she mean it?' I asked. Innocent Linda. She never saw the evil in the hearts and minds of people.

But from that day Dorine picked on me. When I vacuumed the hall, she called me to show me specks I could hardly see and made me vacuum over again. When I cleaned my room, she went in and ran her fingers over the woodwork to show me how much dust I had left behind. 'That ain't the way we do things around here,' she liked to say. 'Do it right or don't do it at all.' As though I had a choice!

'Trying to work me to death, that's what she's doing,' I complained to Linda.

'But why don't you do things right the first time, Gogi?' Linda said. I could only stare at her. My sister!

We had always been close. Linda hadn't minded doing things for me before Dorine came, as long as I read to her. Linda never had time for things like reading. She knew she was pretty and kept trying to make herself perfect. Linda washed her blouses and underwear by hand. She ironed her clothes to defeat even the thought of a wrinkle. And she had always done mine along with hers, just to have me read to her.

But now our stepmother who had turned our father against us had turned my sister against me! Well, if Linda wanted to be a maid, that was her business. I did enough when I vacuumed the

hall and cleaned my room. If Linda had to take Dorine's side against me, then let Dorine read for her. I was satisfied to do my reading – to myself.

Sitting too long on the toilet, I felt the seat cut into my thighs. I got up to unstick myself and leaving the toilet unflushed – not to give away that I had finished – I sat on the closed stool, listening to what ought to have been sounds of glass clinking against glass, of china against china.

The quiet outside the bathroom unsettled me. I usually knew when Linda had finished with the dishes. I always heard when she passed to join Dorine in the living room. They played the television loud, thinking to make me jealous, making me feel unneeded, pretending not to care that I had shut myself from them and that I might go to my room without even a goodnight. But I hadn't heard Linda pass!

The television kept playing. I strained to hear the programme to tell the time. It was on too low. Getting up, I thought of going out to see how things were but sat down again. Better to give Linda a little more time. I started another story.

I had only half finished when my concentration snapped. The television had been turned off. I tried to but couldn't get back into the story. Instead I sat listening, hoping to pick up sounds from the silent house. What time was it?

Getting up, I put my ear to the door. No outside sound. Unlocking the door, I cracked it open and peeked out. The hallway was dark! Everybody had gone to bed! How late was it? Taking off my shoes I started tiptoeing towards my room. Then from the dark behind me I heard: 'Ain't no sense in all that creeping. Them dishes waiting ain't got no ears.' I spun around. A light went on and there she was, lying on a chaise longue that had been pulled up to the living room door. 'That's right, it's me,' she said. 'And it's one o'clock in the morning. Which gives you enough time to wash every dish in the sink squeaking clean before one o'clock noon.'

Tears popped to my eyes as she marched me down past my room, past the room where Linda slept, into the kitchen. Tears kept washing my cheeks as I washed dishes. She sat inspecting every one, acting as though we were playing games. If we were, I expected it to go on forever. She had tricked me – and she had won.

Rosa Guy

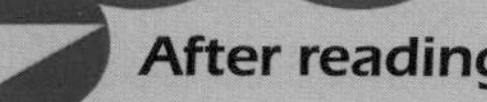

After reading

A

1 Who speaks in the first line of the story:
  a Linda (the sister)?
  b Gogi (the person telling the story)?
  c Dorine (the stepmother)?
2 Where does Gogi escape from doing the washing up?
3 How old is Gogi?
4 What makes Gogi think that Dorine prefers her sister Linda to her?
5 Write down three facts about the father.
6 In what ways are Gogi and Linda different? Try to find two examples.

B

7 Why do you think Gogi dislikes Dorine so much?
8 In the story Gogi reads science fiction stories and fairy tales. Do they suggest anything about her character?
9 Do you find Gogi a likeable character? Or does she behave like a brat? Write about your response to her character.

Extended assignments

1 The story is told from Gogi's point of view. Imagine the same events being told by Dorine. In particular, look at the part of the story when Dorine meets Gogi for the first time. Write Dorine's diary for that evening to show her first impressions of Gogi and Linda, and the way they both behave towards you.
2 In the background of this story is the father. We learn a little about him, but the main focus is on the female characters. Write a character summary of the father. You might mention:
   - what we know about his background
   - his earlier marriage
   - his present life
   - the way he behaves towards Dorine
   - the way he behaves towards his daughters
   - what you like/dislike about him.

Eleanor Farjeon: Grendel the Monster

Genre key: Legend A legend is a popular story from earlier times – such as the stories of Robin Hood, King Arthur and the Knights of the Round Table, or Dick Whittington. Legends are usually rooted in fact – for example, someone called Robin Hood may have actually lived. But the rest of the story has been exaggerated and altered so that it isn't always clear which part is fact and which is fiction. Nowadays we sometimes call someone 'a legend' to show that they have the status of a hero – someone greater than the rest of us.

Before reading

The tale of Beowulf – the hero who fights a monster and its mother – is famous. It is a tale which comes from Scandinavia. There are plenty of different versions around. This one is by Eleanor Farjeon who early in the twentieth century became well-known as a writer of stories and poetry for children. The extract tells the tale of Beowulf's battle underwater with Grendel's mother – the sea-hag ...

Do you already know anything about the Beowulf legend?

Grendel the Monster

Word bank
- bade – asked
- brink – edge
- cutlass – long-bladed knife, often shown in pictures of pirates
- dreary – horrible
- Goths – tribe of Scandinavian people who have come to help the Danes in their battle against Grendel
- Heorot – the great hall where a feast has taken place
- Hrothgar – King of Denmark

Outside in the dark forest lived an old hag, Grendel's mother, at the bottom of a dreary pool. And when Grendel the Monster fled back to her and died, she was filled with rage. That night she came out of her pool and burst into the hall where the Danes and Goths were sleeping; and she fell on Beowulf's dearest friend, killed him, and fled away with his head.

In the morning when all was known, Beowulf cried to Hrothgar: 'Rouse up, guardian of the kingdom! Your men and mine must follow the track of the hag, and whether she hides in the dark forest, in the depths of the earth, or the bottom of the sea, she shall not escape me!'

So the Danes and Goths rode forth from Heorot, and followed Beowulf into the forest; and after a long time they found the dreary pool, and there on the brink of it lay the head of Beowulf's friend. Then the men blew a blast on their horns, and sat down by the pool. At the sound of the blast, strange creatures rose up in the water and swam about: sea-snakes, and water-serpents, and dragons. But they could not make the heart of Beowulf afraid. He put on his armour, bade the men watch for him, and plunged into the pool.

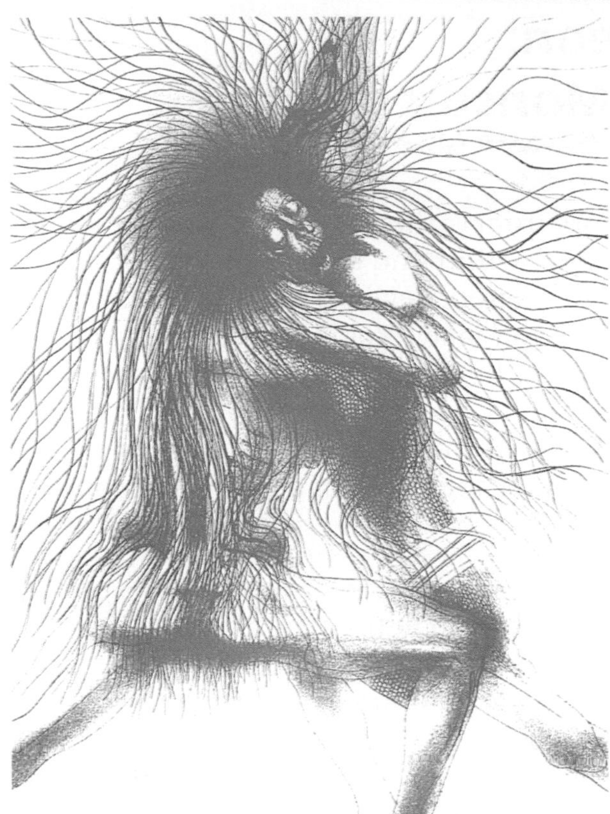

For nine hours the men sat and watched, but Beowulf did not return. Then the Danes would wait no more, but went back sadly to Heorot, to tell the King that Beowulf was dead. But the Goths, who were Beowulf's own men, still waited by the pool.

Now when Beowulf leaped into the pool he began to sink, and the hag, who was waiting for him, seized him and bore him to the bottom. The pool was so deep that it took them the best part of the day. There Beowulf found himself in a strange hall, with a roof that kept off the water, and it was brightly lit with fire. The walls of the hall were hung with mighty weapons, and the floor was strewn with treasures. And further on lay the dead body of Grendel the Monster.

Now Beowulf and the hag began to fight, and Beowulf drew his great sword which had never failed him yet. But strange to tell the sword could not hurt the hag; when it touched her the edge of it turned aside. It was the first time Beowulf's sword had not served him. So he flung the sword away and grappled with the hag with his hands. First he flung her down, and then she rose up and flung him down; but her knife could not cut through his armour any more than his sword could cut through her skin.

Then Beowulf got on his feet again, and he saw amongst the weapons on the wall an old and monstrous cutlass, made for the use of giants. He snatched it from the wall and struck at the hag with it. Instantly she fell, and the fight was ended.

Now Beowulf made ready to return to the top of the pool; but first he picked up his own sword again. He would not take any of the treasure from the hall, the only thing he took was the head of Grendel as a sign that the monster was really dead.

When he came swimming up through the pool, his Goths rejoiced to see him whole and sound. They put the head of Grendel on a pole, and it took four of them to bear it through the forest. And so they marched once more to Heorot with Beowulf in their midst. When they entered Heorot, where the King and Queen sat amongst the Danes, all there were startled at the sight of the head, but were filled with joy because Beowulf was alive.

Then the King rose up and thanked and praised him, calling him his beloved Beowulf. And a new feast was made, and they drank till night drew dim above them, and it was time to sleep again.

Eleanor Farjeon

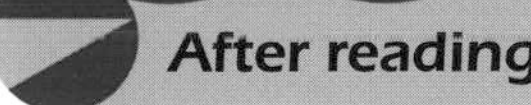

After reading

A

1 Where does the hag live?
2 What crime does the hag commit during the night?
3 Look at these descriptions of Beowulf and the hag. Find four phrases or sentences in the extract, one to fit each statement.
  a Beowulf is courageous.
  b The hag is vicious.
  c Beowulf is an expert warrior.
  d Beowulf is honest.
4 How long do Beowulf's friends wait for him before they give him up as dead?
5 What is the hag's den like? Draw a quick sketch to show what it contains and label the main items.
6 Why does Beowulf take the head of Grendel from the cave?

B

7 What qualities does Beowulf have which make him seem heroic?
8 One reader says: 'I like the extract but I think it would be better if there was more description of the fight between Beowulf and the hag. This would give it more suspense.' Do you agree? In what other ways could the extract have been made more interesting?
9 How can you tell that this is a legend rather than, say, a science fiction tale or ghost story? What makes it feel like a legend? You might mention subject matter, names, vocabulary, etc.

Extended assignments

1 Beowulf is a national hero after killing not one but two monsters. Write the newspaper front page which announces his success. Think of a suitable headline and then write a story of around 200 words. Try to quote Beowulf himself and some of his supporters. You can make up names and comments.
2 The extract makes us feel strongly on Beowulf's side. Have a go at rewriting the text to make the reader sympathetic towards the hag. Some suggestions: give her a name; show her mourning for the death of her only child; make the humans seem aggressive and unreasonable. Then write a descriptive paragraph explaining how you approached the task and how well you feel it has worked.

Sir Thomas Malory: The Death of King Arthur

Advice panel: reading pre-1900 texts

1 Language is always changing. The language we use today will probably seem a bit strange to people in a hundred years' time. Prepare yourself for finding the language of pre-1900 texts unfamiliar and possibly confusing.
2 Focus on what is going on – follow the storyline. Look at the way the characters behave. Don't be put off because there are a few words that are new to you.
3 Try to look for clues about the age of the text – details of places and objects the writer describes (for example the way people are dressed) or words that we no longer use in the same way.

Before reading

This is one of the most famous legends in English. King Arthur is dying and knows he has little time remaining. He asks Sir Bedevere to take his powerful sword Excalibur and to throw it into the lake and then to report what happens. Twice Sir Bedevere tries to deceive the king ...

What do you know about the legend of King Arthur?

How do you think the king will know that Sir Bedevere has not done what he has been told?

Word bank

Avilion – the island paradise where the dying Arthur was taken
brandished – waved
eft – again
haft – handle of a sword or axe
hieth – goes
hoved – pulled
leve – loved
lightly – quickly (as in *light-footedly*)
pommel – rounded end of a sword's handle
slay – kill
tarrying – waiting
wan – become dark
wap – strike (the shore)
weened – imagined

The Death of King Arthur

'My time hieth fast,' said the king. 'Therefore,' said Arthur unto Sir Bedevere, 'take thou Excalibur, my good sword, and go with it to yonder water side, and when thou comest there I charge thee throw my sword in that water, and come again and tell me what thou there seest.'

'My lord,' said Bedevere, 'your commandment shall be done, and lightly bring you word again.'

So Sir Bedevere departed, and by the way he beheld that noble sword, that the pommel and the haft was all of precious stones; and then he said to himself, 'If I throw this rich sword in the water, thereof shall never come good, but harm and loss.' And then Sir Bedevere hid Excalibur under a tree.

And so, as soon as he might, he came again unto the king, and said he had been at the water, and had thrown the sword in the water.

'What saw thou there?' said the king.

'Sir,' he said, 'I saw nothing but waves and winds.'

'That is untruly said of thee,' said the king, 'therefore go thou lightly again, and do my commandment; as thou art to me leve and dear, spare not, but throw it in.'

Then Sir Bedevere returned again, and took the sword in his hand; and then him thought sin and shame to throw away that noble sword, and so eft he hid the sword, and returned again, and told to the king that he had been at the water and done his commandment.

'What saw thou there?' said the king.

'Sir,' he said, 'I saw nothing but the water wap and waves wan.'

'Ah, traitor untrue,' said King Arthur, 'now has thou betrayed me twice. Who would have weened that thou that hast been to me so leve and dear, and thou art named a noble knight, and would betray me for the riches of the sword? But now go again lightly, for thy long tarrying putteth me in great jeopardy of my life, for I have taken cold. And but if thou do now as I bid thee, if ever I may see thee, I shall slay thee mine own hands; for thou wouldst for my rich sword see me dead.'

Then Sir Bedevere departed, and went to the sword, and lightly took it up, and went to the water side; and there he bound the girdle about the hilts, and then he threw the sword as far into the water as he might; and there came an arm and an hand above the water and met it, and caught it, and so shook it thrice and brandished, and then vanished away the hand with the sword in the water. Sir Bedevere came again to the king, and told him what he saw.

'Alas,' said the king, 'help me hence, for I dread me I have tarried over long.'

Then Sir Bedevere took the king upon his back, and so went with him to that water side. And when they were at the water side, even fast by the bank hoved a little barge with many fair ladies in it, and among them all was a queen, and all they had black hoods, and all they wept and shrieked when they saw King Arthur.

'Now put me into the barge,' said the king.

And so he did softly; and there received him three queens with great mourning; and so they set them down, and in one of their laps King Arthur laid his head.

And then that queen said, 'Ah, dear brother, why have ye tarried so long from me? Alas, this wound on your head hath caught over-much cold.'

And so then they rowed from the land, and Sir Bedevere beheld all those ladies go from him.

Then Sir Bedevere cried, 'Ah my lord Arthur, what shall become of me, now ye go from me and leave me here alone among mine enemies?'

'Comfort thyself,' said the king, 'and do as well as thou mayest, for in me is no trust for to trust in; for I will into the vale of Avilion to heal me of my grievous wound: and if thou hear never more of me, pray for my soul.'

But ever the queens and ladies wept and shrieked, that it was a pity to hear. And as soon as Sir Bedevere had lost sight of the barge, he wept and wailed, and so took the forest.

Sir Thomas Malory

After reading

A

1 What does the sword, Excalibur, look like?
2 King Arthur commands Sir Bedevere to throw the sword into the lake. Sir Bedevere disobeys him. What does he do with the sword?
3 Why doesn't he obey the king at first?
4 How does King Arthur know that Sir Bedevere is not telling the truth?
5 What does King Arthur threaten to do to Sir Bedevere after he disobeys him a second time?
6 What happens when Sir Bedevere *does* throw the sword into the lake?

B

7 Pick out a sentence which shows that the extract is written in old-fashioned language. Write the sentence out in modern English. Then write a sentence or two comparing the original with the new version. What are the differences?
8 What makes this text feel like a legend rather than, say, a novel? Try to write a brief paragraph explaining your ideas.

Extended assignments

1 Imagine you had been asked to retell the story for a younger audience – say 5- to 9-year-olds. Write the first part of the legend, making it as lively and clear as you can.
2 Interview Sir Bedevere about why he didn't initially do what he was told by King Arthur. What emotions were going through his mind? What did the sword look like? Why couldn't he bring himself to throw it away? How did he feel when he finally threw it into the lake? As interviewer, ask three to five questions, and give extended paragraph answers.

Ray Bradbury: The House Began to Die

Genre key: Science fiction

It is easy to assume that science fiction can only be about spaceships, alien life, and the world of the future. But science fiction is also about the present – about what science can do to our lives.

The fashion for science fiction stories began in the late nineteenth century, with novels like H G Wells' *The Time Machine*. But by then Mary Shelley had already written about the terrifying dangers of science in her now-classic *Frankenstein*, published in 1818. Science fiction has often taken a negative view of scientific progress – seeing it as something which limits human freedoms and threatens us with destruction.

Before reading

The best science fiction asks the question, 'What if...?' What if Martians invaded Earth? What if a new ice age began? What if robots which are supposed to help us became our enemies? In this extract from a Ray Bradbury tale, technology has taken over the running of a hi-tech house: a voice wakes you up, reminds you what you have to do today, sorts and does the washing, even reads poetry to the people who live there. But how will the house cope with being on fire, with no humans around to help it?

Which science fiction stories (books, programmes, or films) can you think of in which technology runs out of control?

The House Began to Die

Word bank
delicacies – delicious food
faucet – tap
hysterically – without control
linoleum – floor covering
oblivious – not knowing
Picassos and Matisses – priceless paintings by famous artists
psychopathic – crazy
shrapnel – splinters
sublime disregard – not knowing at all

The fire burned on the stone hearth and the cigar fell away into a mound of quiet ash on its tray. The empty chairs faced each other between the silent walls, and the music played.

At ten o'clock the house began to die.

The wind blew. A falling tree-bough crashed through the kitchen window. Cleaning solvent, bottled, shattered over the stove. The room was ablaze in an instant!

'Fire!' screamed a voice. The house lights flashed, water-pumps shot water from the ceilings. But the solvent spread on the linoleum, licking, eating, under the kitchen door, while the voices took up in chorus: 'Fire, fire, fire!'

The house tried to save itself. Doors sprang tightly shut, but the windows were broken by the heat, and the wind blew and sucked upon the fire.

The house gave ground as the fire in ten billion angry sparks moved with flaming ease from room to room and then up the stairs. While scurrying water-rats squeaked from the walls, pistolled their water, and ran for more. And the wall-sprays let down showers of mechanical rain.

But too late. Somewhere, sighing, a pump shrugged to a stop. The quenching rain ceased. The reserve water supply which had filled baths and washed dishes for many quiet days was gone.

The fire crackled up the stairs. It fed upon Picassos and Matisses in the upper halls, like delicacies, baking off the oily flesh, tenderly crisping the canvases into black shavings.

Now the fire lay in beds, stood in windows, changed the colours of drapes!

And then, reinforcements.

From attic trapdoors, blind robot faces peered down with faucet mouths gushing green chemical.

The fire backed off, as even an elephant must at the sight of a dead snake. Now there were twenty snakes whipping over the floor, killing the fire with a clear, cold venom of green froth.

But the fire was clever. It had sent flame outside the house, up through the attic to the pumps there. An explosion! The attic brain which directed the pumps was shattered into bronze shrapnel on the beams.

The fire rushed back into every closet and felt the clothes hung there.

The house shuddered, oak bone on bone, its bared skeleton cringing from the heat, its wire, its nerves revealed as if a surgeon had torn the skin off to let the red veins and capillaries quiver in the scalded air. Help, help! Fire! Run, run! Heat snapped mirrors like the first brittle winter ice. And the voices wailed Fire, fire, run, run, like a tragic nursery rhyme, a dozen voices, high, low, like children dying in a forest, alone, alone. And the voices fading as the wires popped their sheathings like hot chestnuts. One, two, three, four, five voices died.

In the nursery the jungle burned. Blue lions roared, purple giraffes bounded off. The panthers ran in circles, changing colour, and ten million animals, running before the fire, vanished off towards a distant steaming river...

Ten more voices died. In the last instant under the fire avalanche, other choruses, oblivious, could be heard announcing the time, playing music, cutting the lawn by remote-control mower, or setting an umbrella frantically out and in the slamming and opening front door, a thousand things happening, like a clock-shop when each clock strikes the hour insanely before or after the

other, a scene of maniac confusion, yet unity; singing, screaming, a few last cleaning mice darting bravely out to carry the horrid ashes away! And one voice, with sublime disregard for the situation, read poetry aloud in the fiery study, until all the film-spools burned, until all the wires withered and the circuits cracked.

The fire burst the house and let it slam flat down, puffing out skirts of spark and smoke.

In the kitchen, an instant before the rain of fire and timber, the stove could be seen making breakfasts at a psychopathic rate, ten dozen eggs, six loaves of toast, twenty dozen bacon strips, which, eaten by fire, started the stove working again, hysterically hissing!

The crash. The attic smashing into the kitchen and parlour. The parlour into cellar, cellar into sub-cellar. Deep freeze, armchair, film tapes, circuits, beds, and all like skeletons thrown in a cluttered mound deep under.

Smoke and silence. A great quantity of smoke.

Dawn showed faintly in the east. Among the ruins, one wall stood alone. Within the wall, a last voice said, over and over again and again, even as the sun rose to shine upon the heaped rubble and steam:

'Today is August 5, 2026, today is August 5, 2026, today is...'

Ray Bradbury

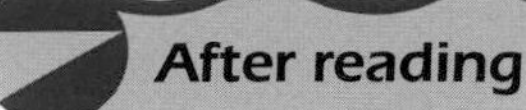

After reading

A

1 What causes the fire to start?
2 Find three things the house does to try to save itself.
3 Find a sentence which makes the fire seem to be alive.
4 Find a sentence which makes the house seem to be alive.
5 How can you tell that the owners of the house must be wealthy?

B

6 As you were reading the story, whose side were you on – the fire's or the house's? Explain why.
7 What do you think the last line of the story means?
8 Which of these sentences feels like the moral or message of the story? Write a sentence explaining your choice:
   a 'Technology can get out of control.'
   b 'It is dangerous to rely on technology.'
   c 'Nature is far more powerful than technology.'
   d 'Firc is cvil.'
   Alternatively, write your own description of the story's message, then explain your thinking behind it.
9 Which two or three of these words would you choose to describe the style of the story? Write about your choices, explaining why you think they are appropriate.

powerful	depressing	disjointed	precise
visual	humorous	poetic	chatty
lively	wordy	simple	fast-moving

Extended assignments

1 Imagine you are the owner of the house away on holiday. You are completely confident in leaving the house because of its high-tech systems and alarms. Imagine what you see and how you feel upon your return. Describe it in as much detail as possible.
2 Imagine the technology of the house *had* managed to defeat the fire. Write the story to show how it might have been different, using all the high-tech gadgets you can think of to help the house save itself.

H G Wells: The War of the Worlds

Before reading

H G Wells was a writer who a century ago pioneered science fiction. This is an extract from his most famous work, *The War of the Worlds*. In the novel, Martians land in Britain and survive by injecting human and animal blood into themselves. Here a battle begins in Chertsey and Shepperton, on the outskirts of London.

The story was written in 1898. What do you expect it to be like?

Word bank
batteries – banks of guns
colossus – giant
concussions – violent blows of the missiles
cowled – hooded, like monks
decapitated – headless
exultation – delight
forthwith – straightaway
hoarse – husky
obliquely – at an angle
pollard – the branches of the tree cut back to encourage future growth
portmanteau – travelling case
reeled – staggered around, spun
simultaneously – at the same time
smote – struck
sojers – (accent) soldiers
yonder – over there

The War of the Worlds

'What's that!' cried a boatman, and 'Shut up, you fool!' said a man near me with a yelping dog. Then the sound came again, this time from the direction of Chertsey, a muffled thud – the sound of a gun.

The fighting was beginning. Almost immediately unseen batteries across the river to our right, unseen because of the trees, took up the chorus, firing heavily one after the other. A woman screamed. Everyone stood arrested by the sudden stir of battle, near us and yet invisible to us. Nothing was to be seen save flat meadows, cows feeding unconcernedly for the most part, and silvery pollard willows motionless in the warm sunlight.

'The sojers 'll stop 'em,' said a woman beside me doubtfully. A haziness rose over the tree-tops.

Then suddenly we saw a rush of smoke far away up the river, a puff of smoke that jerked up into the air, and hung, and forthwith the ground heaved underfoot and a heavy explosion shook the air, smashing two or three windows in the houses near, and leaving us astonished.

'Here they are!' shouted a man in a blue jersey. 'Yonder! D'yer see them? Yonder!'

Quickly, one after the other, one, two, three, four of the armoured Martians appeared, far away over the little trees, across the flat meadows that stretch towards Chertsey, and striding hurriedly towards the river. Little cowled figures they seemed at first, going with a rolling motion and as fast as flying birds.

Then, advancing obliquely towards us, came a fifth. Their armoured bodies glittered in the sun, as they swept swiftly forward upon the guns, growing rapidly larger as they drew nearer. One on the extreme left, the remotest, that is, flourished a huge case high in the air, and the ghostly terrible Heat-Ray I had already seen on Friday night smote towards Chertsey, and struck the town.

At sight of these strange, swift and terrible creatures, the crowd along the water's edge seemed to me to be for a moment horror-struck. There was no screaming or shouting, but a silence. Then a

hoarse murmur and a movement of feet – a splashing from the water. A man, too frightened to drop the portmanteau he carried on his shoulder, swung round and sent me staggering with a blow from the corner of his burden. A woman thrust at me with her hand and rushed past me. I turned, too, with the rush of the people, but I was not too terrified for thought. The terrible Heat-Ray was in my mind. To get under water! That was it!

'Get under water!' I shouted unheeded.

I faced about again, and rushed towards the approaching Martian – rushed right down the gravelly beach and headlong into the water. Others did the same. A boatload of people putting back came leaping out as I rushed past. The stones under my feet were muddy and slippery, and the river was so low that I ran perhaps twenty feet scarcely waist-deep. Then, as the Martian towered overhead scarcely a couple of hundred yards away, I flung myself forward under the surface. The splashes of the people in the boats leaping into the river sounded like thunderclaps in my ears. People were landing hastily on both sides of the river.

But the Martian machine took no more notice for the moment of the people running this way and that than a man would of the confusion of ants in a nest against which his foot has kicked. When, half-suffocated, I raised my head above the water the Martian's hood pointed at the batteries that were still firing across the river, and as it advanced it swung loose what must have been the generator of the Heat-Ray.

In another moment it was on the bank, and in a stride wading half-way across. The knees of its foremost legs bent at the further bank, and in another moment it had raised itself to its full height again, close to the village of Shepperton. Forthwith the six guns, which, unknown to anyone on the right bank, had been hidden behind the outskirts of that village, fired simultaneously. The sudden near concussions, the last close upon the first, made my heart jump. The monster was already raising the case generating the Heat-Ray as the first shell burst six yards above the hood.

I gave a cry of astonishment. I saw and thought nothing of the other four Martian monsters: my attention was riveted upon the near incident. Simultaneously two other shells burst in the air near the body as the hood twisted round in time to receive, but not in time to dodge, the fourth shell.

The shell burst clean in the face of the thing. The hood bulged, flashed, was whirled off in a dozen tattered fragments of red flesh and glittering metal.

'Hit!' shouted I, with something between a scream and a cheer.

I heard answering shouts from the people in the water about me. I could have leapt out of the water with that momentary exultation.

The decapitated colossus reeled like a drunken giant: but it did not fall over. It recovered its balance by a miracle, and no longer heeding its steps, and with the camera that fired the Heat-Ray now rigidly upheld, it reeled swiftly upon Shepperton.

H G Wells

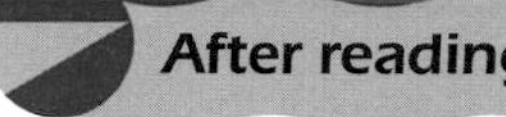

After reading

A

1 What is the first sign that battle is beginning?
2 How do the cows react to the first firing of the guns?
3 What facts do we learn from this extract about the appearance and movement of the Martians? Make a list.
4 In general, how do the people react to the sight of the Martians?
5 The narrator shouts, 'Get under water!' What does this show about his character?
6 Pick out a sentence which best shows the narrator's feelings about the Martians.
7 He feels delighted when the Martian machine is hit at the end of the extract. Does he rejoice too soon? Explain why.

B

8 How does H G Wells make most of the human beings seem foolish?
9 The story was written around a hundred years ago. What clues can you find in the text to suggest its age? Look at:
- descriptions of people and places
- the way people speak
- the writer's style.

10 How does the writer create a feeling of suspense in the first half of the story?

Extended assignments

1 Imagine you were an eyewitness at the battle with the Martians. Write a letter to a friend giving details about what they looked like (you might include a brief illustration based on the information in the text) and how they moved.
2 What do you think happens next? Continue the story. To get started, you might copy H G Wells's last sentence to use as your first.

Jan Mark: Nule

Genre key: Horror

Horror fiction tells the stories of our worst nightmares. Being trapped in a funhouse, trying to escape, being attacked, and everyday creatures (rats, spiders, ants) turning nasty ... these are the special ingredients of the horror story. If they're so unpleasant, why do we read them? Probably because we love to be frightened ... so long as we know it's only a story.

Before reading

Remember trying to get to sleep but something in your house wouldn't let you – a picture on your bedroom wall, the creaking sound of floorboards, the shape of a dressing gown on the back of your door?

Libby and Martin are staying in an old house, full of old-fashioned rooms and features. They notice that the foot of the staircase has a newel-post – a polished wooden post with a rounded ball on top, like a head. Because it looks so much like a person, they call it Nule and dress it with a hat, paper face, long coat and boots. But at night it seems to become too real …

Think of a time when you've been terrified by something at night which by day would have seemed ordinary and not at all frightening.

Nule

Word bank
noble – proud
reckless – without fear

At night the house creaked.

'Thiefly footsteps,' said Libby.

'It's the furniture warping,' said Mum.

Libby thought she said that the furniture was walking, and she could well believe it. The dressing-table had feet with claws; why shouldn't it walk in the dark, tugging fretfully this way and that because the clawed feet pointed in opposite directions? The bath had feet too. Libby imagined it galloping out of the bathroom and tobogganing downstairs on its stomach, like a great white walrus plunging into the sea. If someone held the door open, it would whizz up the path and crash into the front gate. If someone held the gate open, it would shoot across the road and hit the district nurse's car, which she parked under the street light, opposite.

Libby thought of the headlines in the local paper – NURSE RUN OVER BY BATH – and giggled, until she heard the creaks again. Then she hid under the bedclothes.

In his bedroom Martin heard the creaks too, but he had a different reason for worrying. In the attic where the dry rot lurked,

there was a big oak wardrobe full of old dead ladies' clothes. It was directly over his head. Supposing it came through?

Next day he moved his bed.

The vacuum cleaner had lost its casters and had to be helped, by Libby pushing from behind. It skidded up the hall and knocked Nule's football boots askew.

'The Hoover doesn't like Nule either,' said Libby. Although she wouldn't talk to Nule any more she liked talking *about* it, as though that somehow made Nule safer.

'What's that?' said Mum.

'It knocked Nule's feet off.'

'Well, put them back,' said Mum, but Libby preferred not to. When Martin came in he set them side by side, but later they were kicked out of place again. If people began to complain that Nule was in the way, Nule would have to go. He got round this by putting the right boot where the left had been and the left boot on the bottom stair. When he left it, the veil on the hat was hanging down behind, but as he went upstairs after tea he noticed that it was now draped over Nule's right shoulder, as if Nule had turned its head to see where its feet were going.

That night the creaks were louder than ever, like a burglar on hefty tiptoe. Libby had mentioned thieves only that evening, and Mum had said, 'What have we got worth stealing?'

Martin felt fairly safe because he had worked out that if the wardrobe fell tonight, it would land on his chest of drawers and not on him, but what might it not bring down with it? Then he realized that the creaks were coming not from above but from below.

He held his breath. Downstairs didn't creak.

His alarm clock gleamed greenly in the dark and told him that it had gone two o'clock. Mum and Dad were asleep ages ago. Libby would sooner burst than leave her bed in the dark. Perhaps it *was* a burglar. Feeling noble and reckless he put on the bedside lamp, slid out of bed, trod silently across the carpet. He turned on the main light and opened the door. The glow shone out of the doorway and saw him as far as the landing light switch at the top of the stairs, but he never had time to switch it on. From the top of the stairs he could look down into the hall where the street light opposite shone coldly through the frosted panes of the front door.

It shone on the hall-stand where the coats hung, on the blanket chest and the brass jug that stood on it, through the white coins of the honesty plants in the brass jug, and on the broody telephone that never rang at night. It did not shine on Nule. Nule was not there.

Nule was half-way up the stairs, one hand on the banisters and one hand holding up the housecoat, clear of its boots. The veil on the hat drifted like smoke across the frosted glass of the front door. Nule creaked and came up another step.

Martin turned and fled back to the bedroom, and dived under the bedclothes, just like Libby who was three years younger and believed in ghosts.

'Were you reading in bed last night?' said Mum, prodding him awake next morning. Martin came out from under the pillow, very slowly.

'No, Mum.'

'You went to sleep with the light on. *Both* lights,' she said, leaning across to switch off the one by the bed.

'I'm sorry.'

Jan Mark

After reading

A

1 How can you tell that Libby has a vivid imagination?
2 What is Martin most scared of during the first night?
3 What makes the newel post seem alive?
4 How can you tell that the mother is not worried? Try to find two clues.
5 Why were the lights on in Martin's bedroom next morning?
6 At which point does the story begin to get frightening? Choose a sentence where you think the sense of menace begins. Then write a sentence to explain your choice.

B

7 Near the end of the extract, Martin goes to investigate the noises. He thinks he sees Nule moving up the stairs. He runs back to bed. The next sentence is: 'Were you reading in bed last night?' Why do you think the writer suddenly cuts like this to the mother's voice next morning, instead of showing what happened next?
8 How does the writer build up the suspense in the extract? Try to write a short paragraph about what you notice.

Extended assignments

1 Imagine that Libby talks to Martin about what he saw last night on the stairs. Remember that he felt 'noble and reckless', so he may try to cover up his feelings of fear. Write the conversation between them as a script. You could begin it like this:

> **Libby:** (*eager*) So what happened last night?
> **Martin:** (*casual*) What do you mean, what happened?

2 What do you think happens next? Continue the story. You might start at the next evening, as the children go to bed.

Robert Louis Stevenson: The Body Snatcher

Before reading

Horror stories usually deal with subject-matter that terrifies and yet fascinates us. Few writers created more disturbing tales of horror than Robert Louis Stevenson who, late in the nineteenth century, chilled Victorian readers with his tale of Dr Jekyll and Mr Hyde – the polite doctor who by night turns into a menacing monster. Here Stevenson describes another Victorian fascination – the practice of digging up and selling dead bodies for medical experimentation. As medical science developed, trainee surgeons needed human corpses to practise on. Money was to be made by raiding the graveyards at night and selling human remains to certain medical schools.

After a night of drinking with a stranger called Gray, two medical students become involved in grave-robbing, and set out for the body of a farmer's wife …

What is your worst fear or phobia?

Why do you think grave-robbing was so terrifying to readers in the last century?

The Body Snatcher

Word bank

disused radiancy – unfamiliar glow of light
environed – surrounded by
exhumed – uncovered from the earth
formidable – powerful
gig – small horse-drawn carriage
incessant – endless
naught – nothing
plateau – flat land
profundities of the glen – depths of the valley
resonant – echoing
spectral – ghost-like
tragic – sad
traverse – cross
ululations – cries
unhallowed – unholy, evil
venerable – respectable

Somewhat as two vultures may swoop upon a dying lamb, Fettes and Macfarlane were to be let loose upon a grave in that green and quiet resting place. The wife of a farmer, a woman who had lived for sixty years, and been known for nothing but good butter and godly conversation, was to be rooted from her grave at midnight and carried, dead and naked, to that far away city that she had always honoured with her Sunday best; the place beside her family was to be empty till the crack of doom; her innocent and almost venerable members to be exposed to that last curiosity of the anatomist.

Late one afternoon the pair set forth, well wrapped in cloaks and furnished with a formidable bottle. It rained without remission – a cold, dense, lashing rain. Now and again there blew a puff of wind, but these sheets of falling water kept it down.

…It was by this time growing somewhat late. The gig, according to order, was brought round to the door with both lamps brightly shining, and the young men had to pay their bill and take the road. They announced that they were bound for Peebles, and drove in that direction till they were clear of the last houses of the town; then, extinguishing the lamps, returned upon their course, and followed a by-road towards Glencorse. There was no sound but that of their own passage, and the incessant, strident pouring of the

rain. It was pitch dark; here and there a white gate or a white stone in the wall guided them for a short space across the night; but for the most part it was at a foot pace, and almost groping, that they picked their way through that resonant blackness to their solemn and isolated destination. In the sunken woods that traverse the neighbourhood of the burying ground the last glimmer failed them, and it became necessary to kindle a match and re-illumine one of the lanterns of the gig. Thus, under the dripping trees, and environed by huge and moving shadows, they reached the scene of their unhallowed labours.

They were both experienced in such affairs, and powerful with the spade; and they had scarce been twenty minutes at their task before they were rewarded by a dull rattle on the coffin lid. At the same moment Macfarlane, having hurt his hand upon a stone, flung it carelessly above his head. The grave, in which they now stood almost to the shoulders, was close to the edge of the plateau of the graveyard; and the gig lamp had been propped, the better to illuminate their labours, against a tree, and on the immediate verge of the steep bank descending to the stream. Chance had taken a sure aim with the stone. Then came a clang of broken glass; night fell upon them; sounds alternately dull and ringing announced the bounding of the lantern down the bank, and its occasional collision with the trees. A stone or two, which it had dislodged in its descent rattled behind it into the profundities of the glen; and then silence, like night, resumed its sway; and they might bend their hearing to its utmost pitch, but naught was to be heard except the rain, now marching to the wind, now steadily falling over miles of open country.

They were so nearly at an end of their abhorred task that they judged it wisest to complete it in the dark. The coffin was exhumed and broken open; the body inserted in the dripping sack and carried between them to the gig; one mounted to keep it in its place, and the other, taking the horse by the mouth, groped along by the wall and bush until they reached the wider road by the Fisher's Tryst. Here was a faint disused radiancy, which they hailed like daylight; by that they pushed the horse to a good pace and began to rattle along merrily in the direction of the town.

They had both been wetted to the skin during their operations, and now, as the gig jumped among the deep ruts, the thing that stood propped between them fell now upon one and now upon the other. At every repetition of the horrid contact each instinctively repelled it with greater haste; and the process, natural as it was, began to tell upon the nerves of the companions. Macfarlane made some ill-favoured jest about the farmer's wife, but it came hollowly from his lips, and was allowed to drop in silence. Still their unnatural burthen bumped from side to side; and now the

head would be laid, as if in confidence, upon their shoulders, and now the drenching sackcloth would flap icily about their faces. A creeping chill began to possess the soul of Fettes. He peered at the bundle, and it seemed somehow larger than at first. All over the countryside, and from every degree of distance, the farm dogs accompanied their passage with tragic ululations; and it grew and grew upon his mind that some unnatural miracle had been achieved, that some nameless change had befallen the dead body, and that it was in fear of their unholy burthen that the dogs were howling.

'For God's sake,' said he, making a great effort to arrive at speech, 'for God's sake, let's have a light!'

Seemingly Macfarlane was affected in the same direction; for though he made no reply, he stopped the horse, passed the reins to his companion, got down, and proceeded to kindle the remaining lamp. They had by that time got no farther than the crossroad down to Auchendinny. The rain still poured as though the deluge were returning, and it was no easy matter to make a light in such a world of wet and darkness. When at last the flickering blue flame had been transferred to the wick and began to expand and clarify, and shed a wide circle of misty brightness round the gig, it became possible for the two young men to see each other and the thing they had along with them. The rain had moulded the rough sacking to the outlines of the body underneath; the head was distinct from the trunk, the shoulders plainly modelled; something at once spectral and human riveted their eyes upon the ghastly comrade of their drive.

For some time Macfarlane stood motionless, holding up the lamp. A nameless dread was swathed, like a wet sheet, above the body, and tightened the white skin upon the face of Fettes; a fear that was meaningless, a horror of what could not be, kept mounting to his brain. Another beat of the watch, and he had spoken. But his comrade forestalled him.

'That is not a woman,' said Macfarlane, in a hushed voice.

'It was a woman when we put her in,' whispered Fettes.

'Hold that lamp,' said the other. 'I must see her face.'

And as Fettes took the lamp his companion untied the fastenings of the sack and drew down the cover from the head. The light fell very clear upon the dark, well-moulded features and smooth-shaven cheeks of a too familiar countenance, often beheld in dreams of both of these young men. A wild yell rang up into the night; each leaped from his own side into the roadway; the lamp fell, broke, and was extinguished; and the horse, terrified by this unusual commotion, bounded and went off towards Edinburgh at a gallop, bearing along with it, sole occupant of the gig, the body of the dead and long-dissected Gray.

Robert Louis Stevenson

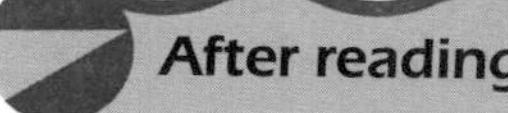

After reading

A

1 What is the weather like?
2 What hint is there in the second paragraph that the men are nervous about their actions?
3 Describe as precisely as you can what the graveyard and its surroundings are like.
4 Look again at the first paragraph. How does the writer make us feel sympathy for the dead wife of the farmer?

B

5 Look at the last 13 lines of the extract (from 'That is not a woman'.) How does the writer build up suspense here?
6 The extract is full of atmosphere. Choose one sentence which you think particularly captures the mood of the night. Then write a sentence or two to say why the sentence is so effective.
7 What clues can you find in the text to show that it was written in the nineteenth century?

Extended assignments

1 How would a newspaper report the recent spate of grave-robbings and, in particular, this unpleasant example? Think of a headline and a 200-word story which informs the readers of what has taken place.
2 How would the text sound if written in our own time? Choose a couple of paragraphs and write them in modern English. Then write a paragraph explaining the changes you have made and how the text feels different.
3 Stevenson's story ends here – but what do you think happens next? The gig is hurtling out of control towards Edinburgh, carrying a body in a sack. It is the body of a man thought to have been killed and dissected some time ago. How has he got there? Is it a ghost, or a trick played by the police? And who is going to be the first to encounter the corpse on the cart …? Continue the story. You might copy the last paragraph of Stevenson's original story to establish the style and setting.

Robert Westall: Rosalie

Genre key: Ghost stories

Ghost stories have a similar effect on us to horror stories – they chill us with fear. What makes them different is that they contain a supernatural element – a ghost or spectre or mysterious being which doesn't belong on earth ... something we thought was dead. Nowadays the differences between the genres can be unclear, but as a rule horror stories – even those with ghosts – are gorier than ghost stories.

Before reading

Robert Westall was well-known for his ghostly tales, as well as for the many other stories he wrote for young readers. In this extract from his short story, *Rosalie,* a class has been talking about the ghost of Rosalie Scott who is supposed to haunt the school...

Think of a ghost story, in a book, television programme, or film, which has had a strong effect on you. What element in it sticks in your mind most? Why do you remember it so well?

Do you think ghost stories are just 'a bit of fun', or could reading too many actually do harm?

Rosalie

It was in maths, on the twenty-first of December, that Tracy Merridew screamed. It was about half-past three in the afternoon and raining, nearly dark outside already. The lights were on in the classroom, but they seemed very far away, high up near the ceiling; and the dull planked floor under the tables was full of dusty shadows.

'For *goodness'* sake,' shouted Miss Hood, 'will you be quiet, Tracy? I am *sick* of this class. I know we break up tomorrow, but today we are *working*!'

But everyone was turning and staring at the dark space beneath the cupboard where the textbooks and the library were kept. The girls were huddling together and the boys were crouching tense, getting ready to be brave. As a whisper went round the room.

'The hand! The hand!'

Then something scuttled with a dry noise, under the cupboard; half-appeared, a dull grey, then vanished again.

'Good God,' said Miss Hood. 'A mouse. Or a rat!'

As she often told them, she was a farmer's daughter, with no time for nonsense. 'We'll soon deal with *that*!' She picked up her heavy blackboard pointer, which she had been known to poke

people with, and made straight for the cupboard. She banged on the side of the cupboard with the pointer, making a terrific din. Hoping to scare the rat out.

Nothing stirred.

Very bravely, or very foolishly, she knelt down and peered underneath, her rather large bottom in its loud check skirt humped up in the air. Still peering, she poked the pointer into the darkness, and rattled it about.

Then she gave such a scream as made Tracy Merridew's seem a squeak.

And collapsed in a dead faint.

And as she lay there a thing like a shrivelled hand, but also like a great thin grey spider, seemed to crawl out from under the cupboard and crawl on to her back; crawl up on to her woolly black jumper. Everyone in the class saw it quite clearly, outlined against Miss Hood's black jumper. So all the rest of their lives they would never forget it...

Everyone started screaming.

Then the classroom door burst open, and Mrs Winterbottom was shouting, 'What is all this nonsense? Miss Hood... Miss Hood!'

And by the time they had got Miss Hood into her chair and splashed her with water, and tried to tell Mrs Winterbottom what had happened, and turned back to the cupboard, the hand was quite gone.

Robert Westall

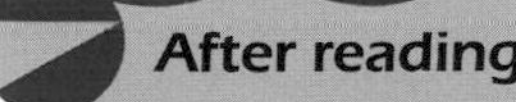

After reading

A

1. Why are the children in the classroom restless?
2. Why does Miss Hood think Tracy Merridew is restless?
3. What does the 'thing' beneath the cupboard look like?
4. What do we learn about Miss Hood's character from the extract? Try to make a list of between three and five points.
5. Look at the first paragraph. Is the atmosphere normal, like just another school afternoon? Or do you think there are hints of trouble? Explain your answer by referring closely to the text.

B

6. At which exact point in the extract do you think it starts to become tense?
7. How does the writer build up the suspense in the extract? Look at: the weather outside; the description of the classroom; Miss Hood's first reaction to 'the hand' compared to the pupils'; the description of the hand itself; the length of sentences and paragraphs.

Extended assignments

1. Imagine you were in the room when the hand moved underneath the cupboard. How would your parent react when you told her or him that night what had happened? Imagine the conversation that might take place, and try to persuade them that it really happened. Set your work out as a script. You could begin like this:

> **Me:** Mum, you'll never believe what happened in maths today.
> **Mum:** (*watching television*) Just switch the volume up a bit, will you?

2. What do you think happens next? When does the hand reappear? Continue the story …

Franz Kafka: The Knock at the Manor Gate

Before reading

Franz Kafka is a Czech writer who is famous for stories which show the isolation and nightmares of human beings – the perfect subject matter for ghost stories.

Most readers agree that this story has suspense, but disagree about whether it is a real ghost story. See what you think...

Word bank
apprehensive – nervous
interrogation – series of questions
manor – a large house
pallet – mattress, often made of straw
proprietor – owner
scrutinized – examined
threshold – border between inside and outside

The Knock at the Manor Gate

It was summer, a hot day. With my sister I was passing the gate of a great house on our way home. I cannot tell now whether she knocked on the gate out of mischief or out of absence of mind, or merely threatened it with her hand and did not knock at all. A hundred paces farther along the road, which here turned to the left, began the village. We did not know it very well, but no sooner had we passed the first house when people appeared and made friendly or warning signs to us; they were themselves apparently terrified, bowed down with terror. They pointed towards the manor house that we had passed and reminded us of the knock on the gate. The proprietor of the manor would charge us with it, the interrogation would begin immediately. I remained quite calm and also tried to calm my sister's fears. Probably she had not struck the door at all, and if she had it could never be proved. I tried to make this clear to the people around us; they listened to me but refrained from passing any opinion. Later they told me that not only my sister, but I too, as her brother, would be charged. I nodded and smiled. We all gazed back at the manor, as one watches a distant smoke-cloud and waits for the flames to appear. And right enough we presently saw horsemen riding in through the wide-open gate. Dust rose, concealing everything, only the tops of the tall spears glittered. And hardly had the troop vanished into the manor courtyard before they seemed to have turned their horses again, for they were already on their way to us. I urged my sister to leave me, I myself would set everything right. I told her that she should at least change, so as to appear in better clothes before these gentlemen.

At last she obeyed and set out on the long road to our home. Already the horsemen were beside us, and even before dismounting they enquired after my sister. She wasn't here at the moment, was the apprehensive reply, but she would come later. The answer was received with indifference; the important thing seemed their having found me. The chief members of the party appeared to be a young lively fellow, who was a judge, and his silent assistant, who was called Assmann. I was commanded to enter the village inn. Shaking my head and hitching up my trousers I slowly began my statement, while the sharp eyes of the party scrutinized me. I still half believed that a word would be enough to free me, a city man, and with honour too, from this peasant folk. But when I had stepped over the threshold of the inn the judge, who had hastened in front and was already awaiting me, said: 'I'm really sorry for this man.' And it was beyond all possibility of doubt that by this he did not mean my present state, but something that was to happen to me. The room looked more like a prison cell than an inn parlour. Great stone flags on the floor, dark, quite bare walls, into one of which an iron rung was fixed, in the middle something that looked half a pallet, half an operating table.

Could I endure any other air than prison air now? That is the great question, or rather it would be if I still had any prospect of release.

Franz Kafka

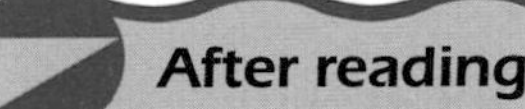

After reading

A

1 Did the narrator's sister definitely knock on the manor door? What does the narrator think?
2 Write a sentence or two saying what we learn about the person who tells the story (the narrator).
3 What are the people in the village like?
4 When people think of ghost stories they expect certain ingredients – haunted houses, someone left on their own, a storm outside, a spirit or ghost … and so on. What ingredients in Franz Kafka's story are typical of ghost stories and which are unusual? Write out a table like this to show your answers (an example is given):

Typical ghost story ingredients	Unusual ingredients
the great manor house – seems like a typical ghost story setting	*a hot summer day – we expect fog or grey skies*

5 The story has appeared in a collection of ghost stories, but one reader in Year 9 said: 'I can't see why this is a ghost story at all.' Do you agree? Explain why you think it is or isn't a ghost story.

B

6 We don't learn the characters' names or anything about their backgrounds. What effect does this have?
7 How does the writer create a feeling of tension in his story?
8 Look again at the final paragraph. Does it make a good ending to the story – full of mystery and hints – or does it disappoint you? Explain your response in as much detail as possible.
9 Some readers have felt that the story has an odd, unfamiliar tone. Write about any parts of the story that felt unusual – either set in a different world or in a different time-period. Give examples from the text to support your ideas.

1 How would the narrator's sister feel about what has happened? Imagine her arrival home and the diary entry she would write. Imagine her confused feelings, her guilt, her wish to change what had happened …
Write her diary entry. You might begin like this:

> Dear Diary,
> I cannot believe what has happened today. One minute my brother and I ...

2 What do you think happens next? Remember that it is (probably!) a ghost story. Continue it, showing what you think takes place. It might help if you write out the final two sentences of Franz Kafka's story to get you going. Write as much as you can. Aim chiefly to give details about:
- the narrator's thoughts and feelings
- the setting
- what happens.

Ruth Rendell: The Clinging Woman

Genre key: Crime fiction Judging by all the detective shows on television, and the number of crime thrillers in bookshops, this seems to be one of our favourite genres. Sometimes we follow the detective in working out 'whodunnit'. In other (usually more modern) stories we may already know who the criminal is. In both types of story, the character of the detective is central to our interest and enjoyment. We usually look at the world through her or his eyes.

Before reading

Ruth Rendell is one of the twentieth century's best-known crime writers, creator of the detective, Inspector Wexford. Sometimes she writes under the name Barbara Vine, when her stories take on a more disturbing style. As Ruth Rendell, she is known for her clever plots and nail-biting suspense.

Look at the title of the story. What do you predict it could be about?

The Clinging Woman

Word bank
anchorage – hold or grip
constituent – ingredient
melodrama – high emotion
pensively – thoughtfully
profound – deep
St George – hero and patron saint of England, who killed the dragon

The girl was hanging by her hands from the railings of a balcony. The balcony was on the twelfth floor of the high-rise block next to his. His flat was on the ninth floor and he had to look up to see her. It was half-past six in the morning. He had been awakened by the sound of an aircraft flying dangerously low overhead, and had got out of bed to look. His sleepy gaze, descending from the blue sky which was empty of clouds, empty of anything but the bright vanishing arrow of the aircraft, alighted – at first with disbelief – on the hanging figure.

He really thought he must be dreaming, for this sunrise time was the hour for dreams. Then, when he knew he wasn't, he decided it must be a stunt. This was to be a scene in a film. There were cameramen down there, a whole film unit, and all the correct safety precautions had been taken. Probably the girl wasn't even a real girl, but a dummy. He opened the window and looked down. The car park, paved courts, grass spaces between the blocks, all were deserted. On the balcony rail one of the dummy's hands moved, clutching its anchorage more tightly, more desperately. He had to believe then what was obviously happening – unbelievable only because melodrama, though a frequent constituent of real life, always is. The girl was trying to kill herself.

She had lost her nerve and was now trying to stay alive. All these thoughts and conclusions of his occupied about thirty seconds. Then he acted. He picked up the phone and dialled the emergency number for the police.

The arrival of the police cars and the ultimate rescue of the girl became the focus of gossip and speculation for the tenants of the two blocks. Someone found out that it was he who had alerted the police and he became an unwilling hero. He was a modest, quiet young man, and, disliking this limelight, was relieved when the talk began to die away, when the novelty of it wore off, and he was able to enter and leave his flat without being pointed at as a kind of St George and sometimes even congratulated.

About a fortnight after that morning of melodrama, he was getting ready to go to the theatre, just putting on his overcoat, when the doorbell rang. He didn't recognize the girl who stood outside. He had never seen her face.

She said, 'I'm Lydia Simpson. You saved my life. I've come to thank you.'

His embarrassment was acute. 'You shouldn't have,' he said with a nervous smile. 'You really shouldn't. That's not necessary. I only did what anyone would have done.'

She was calm and tranquil, not at all his idea of a failed suicide. 'But no one else did,' she said.

'Won't you come in? Have a drink or something?'

'Oh, no, I couldn't think of it. I can see you're just going out. I only wanted to say thank you very, very much.'

'It was nothing.'

'Nothing to save someone's life? I'll always be grateful to you.'

He wished she would either come in or go away. If this went on much longer the people in the other two flats on his floor would hear, would come out, and another of those bravest-deeds-of-the-year committee meetings would be convened. 'Nothing at all,' he said desperately. 'Really, I've almost forgotten it.'

'I shall never forget, never.'

Her manner, calm yet intense, made him feel uncomfortable and he watched her retreat into the lift – smiling pensively – with profound relief. Luckily, they weren't likely to meet again. The curious thing was that they did, the next morning at the bus stop.

Ruth Rendell

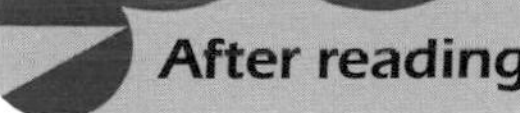

After reading

A

1 Why had the man gone to his balcony at this unusual hour in the first place?

2 When he first sees the girl clinging there, how does he try to explain it?

3 Write down three facts we learn about the man and two about the girl.

4 Why for a while was the man 'pointed at as a kind of St George'?

5 Do you think the man is proud of the way he reacted to the 'clinging woman'? Or does he simply want to forget about it? Explain your answer.

B

6 Look again at the first paragraph. Notice all the pronouns Ruth Rendell uses – 'her', 'he', and 'his'. We don't learn anything about the characters' names. Why do you think this is? And why do you think Ruth Rendell avoids telling us the name of the main character, the narrator, in the extract as a whole?

7 How well does this extract work as the opening of a crime story? How could it be made more tense or interesting or unpredictable? Explain your ideas.

Extended assignments

1 How would the extract work as the opening for a television crime drama? Design a storyboard to show how the story might develop frame by frame. Don't spend too much time on the illustrations – it's the narrative sequence which is most important. Use dialogue in speech bubbles and add labels to clarify your ideas if you wish. Then write a paragraph explaining:

- how you approached the task
- what changes you made to the story (if any)
- what problems you faced
- whether you are pleased with the finished storyboard.

2 The story is written in the third-person mode, making the reader more distant from what is going on – 'He … he … him'. How would the story work if told in first-person mode by the man himself (i.e. 'I … I … me')? Try rewriting this opening from the man's point-of-view, and then write a paragraph explaining the problems you encountered and how the text feels different overall.

3 What do you think happens next? Is the girl as innocent as we first think, or do you find her quite sinister? What was her purpose in using this balcony for her suicide attempt – and was it a genuine attempt anyway …? Continue the story.

Arthur Conan Doyle: The Engineer's Thumb

Before reading

The fashion for reading crime fiction began in the late nineteenth century with writers like Edgar Allan Poe and Wilkie Collins. Charles Dickens' final, unfinished book was a crime story called *The Mystery of Edwin Drood* – a sign of how popular the genre had become.

Most famous of all the early detectives is Sherlock Holmes. Here, his sidekick Dr Watson opens his surgery door to two mysterious and gristly visitors ...

What do you know about Sherlock Holmes and Dr Watson?

The Engineer's Thumb

Word bank
abode – home
agitation – nervousness, worry
carafe – glass bottle for water
carbolized – disinfected, to help the wound to heal
cleaver – large knife for chopping meat
hansom – horse-drawn cab
hydraulics – branch of engineering concerned with water-power
monotonous – boring
Paddington – London railway station
province – area of expertise
tout – somebody who brings customers to a business
trivial – unimportant
tweed – thick woollen cloth

One morning, at a little before seven o'clock, I was awakened by the maid tapping at the door, to announce that two men had come from Paddington, and were waiting in the consulting-room. I dressed hurriedly, for I knew by experience that railway cases were seldom trivial, and hastened downstairs. As I descended, my old ally, the guard, came out of the room, and closed the door tightly behind him.

'I've got him here,' he whispered, jerking his thumb over his shoulder; 'he's all right.'

'What is it, then?' I asked, for his manner suggested that it was some strange creature which he had caged up in my room.

'It's a new patient,' he whispered. 'I thought I'd bring him round myself; then he couldn't slip away. There he is, all safe and sound. I must go now, Doctor, I have my dooties, just the same as you.' And off he went, this trusty tout, without even giving me time to thank him.

I entered my consulting-room, and found a gentleman seated by the table. He was quietly dressed in a suit of heather tweed, with a soft cloth cap, which he had laid down upon my books. Round one of his hands he had a handkerchief wrapped, which was mottled all over with bloodstains. He was young, not more than five-and-twenty, I should say, with a strong masculine face; but he was exceedingly pale, and gave me the impression of a man who was suffering from some strong agitation, which it took all his strength of mind to control.

'I am sorry to knock you up so early, Doctor,' he said. 'But I have had a very serious accident during the night. I came in by train this morning, and on enquiring at Paddington as to where I

might find a doctor, a worthy fellow very kindly escorted me here. I gave the maid a card, but I see that she has left it upon the side table.'

I took it up and glanced at it. 'Mr Victor Hatherley, hydraulic engineer, 16a Victoria Street, (3rd Floor).' That was the name, style, and abode of my morning visitor. 'I regret that I have kept you waiting,' said I, sitting down in my library chair. 'You are fresh from a night journey, I understand, which is in itself a monotonous occupation.'

'Oh, my night could not be called monotonous,' said he, and laughed. He laughed very heartily, with a high ringing note, leaning back in his chair, and shaking his sides. All my medical instincts rose up against that laugh.

'Stop it,' I cried. 'Pull yourself together!' And I poured some water from a carafe.

It was useless, however. He was off in one of those hysterical outbursts which come upon a strong nature when some great crisis is over and gone. Presently he came to himself once more, very weary and blushing hotly.

'I have been making a fool of myself,' he gasped.

'Not at all. Drink this!' I dashed some brandy into the water, and the colour began to come back to his bloodless cheeks.

'That's better!' said he. 'And now, Doctor, perhaps you would kindly attend to my thumb, or rather to the place where my thumb used to be.'

He unwound the handkerchief and held out his hand. It gave even my hardened nerves a shudder to look at it. There were four protruding fingers and a horrid red spongy surface where the thumb should have been. It had been hacked or torn right from the roots.

'Good heavens!' I cried, 'this is a terrible injury. It must have bled considerably.'

'Yes, it did. I fainted when it was done; and I think that I must have been senseless for a long time. When I came to, I found that it was still bleeding, so I tied one end of my handkerchief very tightly round the wrist, and braced it up with a twig.'

'Excellent! You should have been a surgeon.'

'It is a question of hydraulics, you see, and came within my own province.'

'This has been done,' said I, examining the wound, 'by a very heavy and sharp instrument.'

'A thing like a cleaver,' said he.

'An accident, I presume?'

'By no means.'

'What, a murderous attack!'

'Very murderous indeed.'

'You horrify me.'

I sponged the wound, cleaned it, dressed it; and, finally, covered it with cotton wadding and carbolized bandages. He lay back without wincing, though he bit his lip from time to time.

'How is that?' I asked, when I had finished.

'Capital! Between your brandy and your bandage, I feel a new man. I was very weak, but I have had a good deal to go through.'

'Perhaps you had better not speak of the matter. It is evidently trying to your nerves.'

'Oh, no; not now. I shall have to tell my tale to the police; but, between ourselves, if it were not for the convincing evidence of this wound of mine, I should be surprised if they believed my statement, for it is a very extraordinary one, and I have not much in the way of proof with which to back it up. And, even if they believe me, the clues which I can give them are so vague that it is a question whether justice will be done.'

'Ha!' cried I, 'if it is anything in the nature of a problem which you desire to see solved, I should strongly recommend you to come to my friend Mr Sherlock Holmes before you go to the official police.'

'Oh, I have heard of that fellow,' answered my visitor, 'and I should be very glad if he would take the matter up, though of course I must use the official police as well. Would you give me an introduction to him?'

'I'll do better. I'll take you round to him myself.'

'I should be immensely obliged to you.'

'We'll call a cab and go together. We shall just be in time to have a little breakfast with him. Do you feel equal to it?'

'Yes. I shall not feel easy until I have told my story.'

'Then my servant will call a cab, and I shall be with you in an instant.' I rushed upstairs, explained the matter shortly to my wife, and in five minutes was inside a hansom, driving with my new acquaintance to Baker Street.

Arthur Conan Doyle

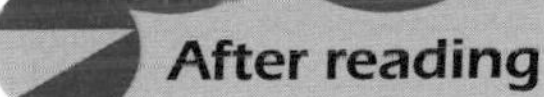

After reading

A

1 Which of these statements best describes why Dr Watson rushes in the first paragraph?

- **a** because he is late
- **b** because there is a knock at the door
- **c** because he knows that railway accidents are often serious
- **d** because he expects trouble.

2 Two men are waiting for Dr Watson. How can you tell that he knows one of them?

3 What has happened to the 'victim'?

4 Why has the injury been so well bandaged?

5 How would you describe Dr Watson in the extract:

calm	decisive	surprised	upset	rude

Write a sentence to explain your choice.

B

6 Do you find anything surprising about Dr Watson's response to the injury?

7 What sort of person do you think the victim is?

8 What clues can you find that the story is set in the nineteenth century? Look in particular at the words the writer uses and the dialogue between the characters.

Extended assignments

1 What do you think happens next? Continue the story with the visit to Sherlock Holmes. Try to keep the style of the story going as much as you can.

2 The extract contains a number of words and phrases which show when it was set. How would the story work if it was updated to the present day? For example, a phrase like 'he... gave me the impression of a man who was suffering from some strong agitation' might become: 'he looked deeply worried'. Choose a section of the story and try writing it in a more modern form of English. Then, in an accompanying paragraph, explain what changes you made and how the overall effect differs from the original version.

DRAMA

Reading and responding to drama texts

This section contains a range of drama texts, including:
- play extracts from this century and from the past
- drama from different countries (for example, Norway, the USA, Britain)
- extracts as well as whole texts
- texts designed to show different genres or categories of writing – such as stage plays, monologues, comedy sketches, and so on.

Many students say that one of their favourite activities in English lessons is reading plays aloud. Getting a part, looking through your lines, reading it in front of the class – these can be exciting, as well as nerve-racking, experiences. In the process, you improve your skills in reading aloud, perfect your timing, learn to use your voice to express a character's emotions, and gain confidence in public performance.

Reading drama scripts can also be a confusing activity, especially if you're expected to read them on your own. They can feel disjointed, or broken up, and it can be difficult to follow who's saying what.

This section gives you practice in reading drama. Whether you read the extracts aloud as a group, or individually in your head, you'll develop your familiarity with the layout and language of different types of drama.

Key skills

- Gaining confidence in reading aloud.
- Following what happens in a drama text.
- Looking at the way drama texts are structured.
- Looking at features like characterization and setting.
- Examining different writers' styles.
- Learning more about genres (categories of drama).

Dawn French and Jennifer Saunders: Health Expert

Advice panel: reading drama texts

1 Try to bring the text alive in your head. Imagine the characters in the setting speaking to one another. Try to imagine where they are, what they look like, how they speak. Use the writer's stage directions to help you get a clearer sense of what things look like.

2 Don't read too quickly. Drama texts probably need to be read more slowly than other forms. You need to concentrate, too, so that you can remember who is speaking to whom.

3 Remember that a drama text is intended for actors and directors. Put yourself in their shoes. How would *you* play this part? How would you direct the scene? What would it look like on stage? How would you use lighting and scenery to make it come to life? Don't be afraid of giving your opinion.

Genre key: Comic sketch

Many comedy programmes are built around a series of comic sketches. These usually last from just a few seconds to three or four minutes. A sketch has a simple purpose: to entertain us. So don't expect lots of description or detail. Skilful sketch-writers set the scene very quickly and get on with their serious business – of making us laugh.

Before reading

You may already have seen some of the comedy routines of Dawn French and Jennifer Saunders. They are well-known for their comedy sketch shows, often featuring parodies or 'send-ups' of famous films, music videos, or television programmes. This sketch is an example of the way they make us laugh at other programmes.

Are you a fan of French and Saunders? Which of their sketches do you remember best? Who do you think their work appeals to most – younger or older people, women or men?

Word bank

epidemic – widespread disease
gangrene – a disease which eats away at the flesh
organic food – food grown without use of artificial substances, such as pesticides
perennial – long-lasting, eternal (i.e. the sort of expert who 'always' seems to be on TV)
TV AM – the television company that until the early 1990s provided ITV's breakfast television programmes

Health Expert

(TV AM set – large sofa. **Jennifer** *is the interviewer,* **Dawn** *the perennial 'expert'. They never know quite which camera is on.)*

Jennifer: Welcome back. On the sofa with me today is our resident Health Expert, Dawn French. I'm going to be asking her what's good for our health and what's bad. Dawn, hello.
Dawn: Hello.
Jennifer: So, tell us, Dawn, what is good for our health and what is bad?
Dawn: Things that are generally good for our health are: breathing, walking and reacting to sudden light by blinking.
Jennifer: And what's bad for our health?
Dawn: Bad for our health? Well, heart attacks, comas and gangrene. All of these things are bad for our health.

Jennifer: Can I just say to viewers, we're not trying to make a point here. We're not trying to say anything this morning. That's very interesting, we've been literally flooded with letters asking us what we can and can't eat.

(**Dawn** *picks up basket of fruit from side of her.)*

Dawn: Well, of course, the easy guideline to what we can eat is anything that's edible, for instance Smarties are edible.

Jennifer: Well, that's all very well, but many people are puzzled about what *not* to eat.

Dawn: You'd be surprised at the things that are bad to eat, metal, concrete, wood, don't eat trousers and please, please don't eat instant noodles.

Jennifer: I see, we're surrounded by things we can't eat. Obviously it's very difficult for some of our viewers to make the right decisions with regards to food when faced with *so* much choice. What can they do?

Dawn: My tip is take advice about this from experts. When you're in a food shop, take food from the shelf, hold it up to the assistant and simply ask, 'Excuse me, is this edible?'

Jennifer: Well, I hope that's clarified this murky area and let's all look forward to a happier and healthier life as a result of our little chat here.

Dawn: Do you want to know anything about organic food?

Jennifer: No, that's a bit complicated and political for our viewers. OK, lovely, this is rather nice. (*Touching the food hamper.*)

Dawn: The thing is, a lot of our viewers would simply throw the fruit out of this basket and try to eat the basket.

Jennifer: Is it an epidemic?

Dawn: Not at the moment.

Dawn French and Jennifer Saunders

After reading

A

1. The directions at the start of the sketch say: 'They never know quite which camera is on'. How would the actors behave to show this?
2. Jennifer begins by saying, 'Welcome back'. What does she mean?
3. What do you think Jennifer means when she says, 'Can I just say to viewers, we're not trying to make a point here. We're not trying to say anything this morning'?
4. Find an example which shows that the presenters don't think the viewers are very clever.

B

5 How do you think the two presenters should look? How should they sit? How much should they look at each other? How much at the camera? Should they smile or be serious? Write a paragraph about the way they should play their roles.

6 What makes the sketch funny? How would you make it more humorous? Are there any parts of it which, for you, don't work?

Extended assignments

1 Watch two students in your class perform the sketch, and write down notes on what they could do to improve the way it works. Then watch them perform it again, after they have listened to the comments of people in the class. What further advice would you give them?
Take your notes, and write an advice sheet for actors playing the sketch. You might use headings like these:
- sitting position
- facial expression
- eye-contact
- speaking the lines

2 Write another sketch for French and Saunders, again for their 'breakfast TV' slot. This time make Dawn French the fitness or education expert. Set your script out exactly like the 'Health Expert' script.

Joyce Grenfell: Going Home Time

Genre key: Monologue In drama texts we are used to reading dialogue – talk between two or more characters. Some drama uses the structure of monologue – one person talking – to allow us to see inside the mind of a character.

Before reading

Joyce Grenfell, an actress famous for her roles in *St Trinians* and early *Carry On* films, wrote a variety of monologues, belonging to all kinds of characters. Some monologues show the inner thoughts of a character – what she is thinking, hoping, worrying about, and so on. In this monologue, however, we hear just what the character says, but not what others around her say – a bit like listening to one half of a telephone conversation.

This monologue features one of Joyce Grenfell's best known creations – the primary school teacher for whom nothing quite goes right …

Going Home Time

Word bank
puggy – like a monkey's
wee mite – (dialect) little thing

(*It is winter.*)

Children – it's time to go home, so finish tidying up and put on your hats and coats. Some of our mummies are here for us, so hurry up.

Billy won't be long, Mrs Binton. He's on hamster duty.

Now let's see if we can't all help each other.

Janey – I said help each other. Help Bobbie carry that chair, don't pin him against the wall with it.

We're having a go at our good neighbour policy here, Mrs Binton, but it doesn't always …

Neville, off the floor, please. Don't lie there.

And Sidney, stop painting, please.

Because it's time to go home.

Well, you shouldn't have started another picture, should you. What is it this time?

Another blue man! Oh, I see, so it is.

All right, you can make it just a little bit bluer, but only one more brushful, please, Sidney.

We don't think he's very talented, but we feel it's important to encourage their self-expression. You never know where it might lead…

Rachel. Gently – help Teddy *gently* into his coat.

It's a lovely coat, Teddy, what's wrong with it?

Oh. It looks like a boy's coat when you wear it. And lots of boys wear pink.

Poor wee mite, he has three older sisters!

Neville, I said get up off the floor.

Who shot you dead?

David did? Well, I don't suppose he meant to.

He may have meant to then, but he doesn't mean it now, and anyhow I say you can get up.

No, don't go and shoot David dead, because it's time to go home.

George. What did I tell you not to do? Well, don't do it.

And Sidney, don't wave that paint-brush about like that, you'll splash somebody. LOOK OUT, DOLORES!

Sidney!... It's all right, Dolores, you aren't hurt, you're just surprised. It was only a nice soft brush. But you'd better go and wash your face before you go home.

Because it's all blue.

Sidney, I saw you deliberately put that paint-brush up Dolores's little nostril.

No, it wasn't a jolly good shot. It was... I don't want to discuss it, Sidney.

Now go and tell Dolores you're sorry.

Yes, now.

Thank you, Hazel, for putting the chairs straight for me.

You are a great helper.

Thank you.

And thank you, Dicky, for closing the cupboard door for me.

Dicky, is there somebody *in* the cupboard?

Well, let her out at once.

Are you all right, Peggy? What did you go into the cupboard for?

But we don't have mices – I mean mouses – in our toy cupboard. Mouses only go where there is food, and we don't have any food in our toy cupboard.

When did you hide a bicky in there?

Every day!

Well, perhaps we have got mices in our toy cupboard. I'll have to look.

No, you go and get your coat on.

Dicky – We never shut people in cupboards.

Because they don't like it.

What do you mean, she's puggy? Peggy's puggy?

Oh, she's got puggy hands. But you don't have to hold her hand...

Well, you must ask her nicely to let go.

Well, if she won't let go...

You'll have to work it out for yourself, Dicky.

Edgar and Timmy – your knitted caps are not for playing tug-of-war with. Look, now the pom-pom's come off.

Whose is it?

Well, give it back to Sidney.

Where are your caps?

Well, go and ask Sidney to give them back to you.

Turn round, Geoffrey. You've got your wellingtons on the wrong feet.

Yes, you have. You'll have to take them off and start again.

Why can't you reach?

Well, undo your coat and then you can bend. Take off your woolly gloves.

And your scarf.

You can keep your balaclava on. How many jerseys are you wearing?

Heavens. No wonder you can't bend.

Caroline, come and help Geoffrey.

Don't kick her, Geoffrey. She's come to help.

Sidney, I told you to put that paint-brush down... LOOK OUT, DOLORES!

Well, *that* wasn't a very good shot, was it? You didn't mean to put it in her ear, did you?

Well, you shouldn't have.

You're all right, Dolores. It was just a bit of a surprise, but you'll have to go and wash again.

Because you've got a blue ear.

Sidney, I'm ashamed of you, a big boy of four, and she's only three.

And Sidney, what have you done with Timmy and Edgar's caps?

No, I'm not going to guess.

And I don't want to know they are hidden in a special secret place, I want to know exactly where they are.

No, I'm not going to try and find them. You're going to tell me where they are.

Well, go and get them out of the waste-paper basket at oncc. Waste-paper baskets aren't for putting caps in.

Now go and say you are sorry to Dolores.

Yes, again.

We think his aggression is diminishing, but we do have setbacks.

Lavinia, is that your coat you've got on? It looks so enormous.

Oh, you're going to grow into it. I see.

Hazel, thank you for helping Betty into her jacket.

Just zip her up once. Not up and down.

No, Neville, you can't have a turn.

No, children, you can't all zip Betty.

Jenny, come here.

Jenny, when we have paid a visit to the littlest room, what do we do?

We pull our knickers up again.

Goodbye, Hazel, Goodbye, Bobbie. Goodbye, everybody.

Goodbye, Mrs Binton.

Hurry up, Sidney, because you'll keep your Mummy waiting.

Well, your Granny then.

Somebody is coming to take you away, aren't they, Sidney?

Good.

No, you won't see me tomorrow, Sidney.

Tomorrow is Saturday, thank heaven.

Joyce Grenfell

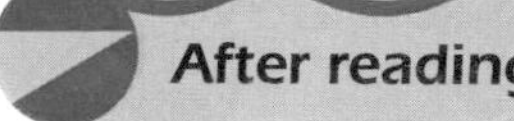

A

1 Use this table to sort out what the different children do during the monologue. To make it easier, you simply need to write a number against a letter – for example, 1C or 3F.

1 Billy	**A** lies on the floor
2 Janey	**B** pretends to shoot people
3 Neville	**C** doesn't dress properly after going to the toilet
4 Teddy	**D** pins Bobbie against the wall with a chair
5 David	**E** puts the chairs straight
6 Sidney	**F** can't put his boots on
7 Jenny	**G** causes trouble with a paintbrush
8 Geoffrey	**H** hamster duty
9 Hazel	**I** locks someone in the cupboard
10 Dicky	**J** feels embarrassed about his coat

2 One pupil causes a lot more trouble than any other. Which one? Write down the name and then explain your choice in a sentence.

3 Who do you think Mrs Binton might be?

4 Choose two words which you think best sum up the character of the teacher. After each word, write a sentence explaining why you think it is so suitable.

angry	weak	caring	helpful	irritated	tired
upset	patient	impatient	strict	good-humoured	

5 Look at the last two lines of the monologue. Is it true that the teacher doesn't like her job? Explain your answer in a sentence or two.

B

6 Look again at some of the names of the children: Lavinia, Sidney, Neville, Geoffrey. What impression do you get from the names? What do they tell you either about the school, or about when the monologue was written?

7 The teacher talks in one style to the children. She talks differently to Mrs Binton. Explain how her style changes and why.

8 How much does the text remind you of real primary schools? What feels right in it, and what feels exaggerated?

1 Imagine it is the first time Mrs Binton has been inside the classroom at the end of school. What impression does she get? Does she like what she sees or does she disapprove? Imagine she goes home and telephones a friend about the atmosphere in the classroom and the behaviour of the teacher and children. Write the conversation between Mrs Binton and her friend.

2 What overall impression do we get of the primary school teacher? Think about:
- her behaviour and attitude towards the children
- the way she speaks to them
- the way she speaks to Mrs Binton
- her final remarks about the weekend.

Write a character study describing what the school teacher is like, and what you like/dislike about her.

Michael Wilcox: Last Bus to Woodstock

Before reading

Watching films or television drama, we can easily forget that everything on screen began life as written ideas on a page. This extract is the opening sequence from an episode of *Inspector Morse* – a highly popular detective series on ITV. The sequence includes the opening titles – the words that come up on screen to tell viewers what they are watching. The episode is called 'Last Bus to Woodstock'.

What do you know about the *Inspector Morse* series? Have you seen any episodes? Do you know any of the actors who star in it? If you have watched it, what do you think of it?

Last Bus to Woodstock

Word bank
don – someone who teaches at Oxford or Cambridge University
hitch – thumb a lift
humiliated – deeply embarrassed
Woodstock – village to the north of Oxford

1 EXTERIOR. OXFORD ROAD: BUS STOP. NIGHT.

It is 6.45pm. It is dark and starting to rain. Sylvia Kane, in her late teens and fashionably dressed in a yellow raincoat, approaches a bus stop at which an elderly lady, Miss Jarman, is waiting for the bus. Another woman, whose identity we do not see, runs up behind Sylvia. (It is, in fact, Sue Widdowson, a nurse.)

SYLVIA Oh, hello. I'm off to Woodstock. You coming too? Great!

During this Sue responds silently with nods and body language.

Titles.

2 EXTERIOR. OXFORD ROAD. BUS STOP. NIGHT.

As the rain falls harder, the two women cover themselves up as best they can. Sylvia has her jacket over her head and Sue has the hood of her anorak up. Sylvia has trotted well ahead of Sue and approaches Miss Jarman.

SYLVIA Excuse me. When's the next bus, please?
MISS JARMAN Supposed to be here soon. It's generally late.

Titles.

3 EXTERIOR. OXFORD ROAD. NIGHT.

Sylvia calls to Sue…

SYLVIA Why don't we hitch ?

Titles.

4 INTERIOR. THE FOX AND CASTLE. NIGHT.

The public bar of The Fox and Castle pub in Woodstock. It is getting crowded, even though it is still quite early in the evening. John Sanders, in his late teens, enters. He looks unsure of himself. He finds his way to the bar and is about to order when Peter Newlove, a handsome don, pushes in front of him.

NEWLOVE Pint of best, please.

Vikki, the barmaid, serves him. John Sanders look humiliated.

Titles.

5 EXTERIOR. OXFORD ROAD. NIGHT.

A red Ford Escort, driven by a man, (Bernard Crowther), has stopped to pick up the hitching Sylvia Kane. Sue is some yards behind Sylvia. The car door opens and Sylvia hops in, shutting her door. Sue catches sight of the driver, who doesn't see her. The car drives off, leaving her behind. She turns back to the bus stop and sees the bus approaching. She joins Miss Jarman, who hardly notices her, and gets on the bus. Note: The rear nearside lights of the car are broken.

Titles.

6 INTERIOR. THE FOX AND CASTLE. NIGHT.

In the bar of The Fox and Castle John Sanders is still on his own, on a stool at the bar. He is trying to get another pint. He holds up his empty glass shyly, but Vikki is talking to Peter Newlove. She looks as though she is being chatted up and is enjoying it. She sees Sanders and goes over to him.

VIKKI Same again, love?
SANDERS Yes, please.

She pulls another pint. Newlove leaves the bar.

VIKKI On your own?
SANDERS Supposed to be meeting someone. She's a bit late.
VIKKI Well, it's a pretty nasty night out there.

Vikki gives him the pint and takes his money. Sanders suddenly gets off his stool.

SANDERS Back in a minute!

After reading

A

1 What do we learn from this opening sequence about the different characters – their ages, appearance, behaviour? Use the prompts below to fill in details about four of the characters:

Sylvia
last name:
rough age:
appearance:
what she does in the extract:

Miss Jarman:
rough age:
what she does in the extract:

Sue Widdowson:
appearance:
what she does in the extract:

John Sanders:
rough age:
behaviour:
what he does in the extract:

2 Do you think Sylvia and Sue know one another?
3 What do you think is going to happen in the next few minutes of the episode?
4 Which characters do you think will be most important in the episode? Try to explain why.

B

5 How does the writer build up a feeling of suspense in the extract?
6 The story is broken up. One scene suddenly switches to another (from the road to the pub and then back again). It is also broken up by the titles. What effect does this have?
7 The writer, Michael Wilcox, has said that he wanted to make sure that viewers didn't 'zap the programme' by switching channels just as the programme started. He wanted to get them interested in the story as quickly as possible. How well do you think he achieves his aim? Explain your response.

1 Screenplays tell their stories through pictures as well as words. How would the *Inspector Morse* opening sequence be different as the opening of a novel? (Remember that many of the original stories did begin as novels by Colin Dexter.) Try rewriting the extract as if it were the opening page or two of a crime novel. You might begin like this:

> 'The night grew darker as the rain fell more violently. It was only 6.45pm, but it might have been midnight. At a bus stop on a lonely road ...'

2 Screenplays for films and television drama tell their stories by cutting from one scene to another, as well as through words. Choose two locations from the list below and try to write your own gripping opening sequence that viewers won't want to 'zap'. Make up some characters for the viewer to follow in each scene, as Michael Wilcox does in his *Morse* episode.

- country lane
- inside sports centre
- in front of an ice-cream van
- on a beach
- someone sitting at a computer in a deserted office

Louis Phillips: Carwash

Genre key: Stage play Stage drama is one of the oldest genres in the world. Before people could read, they would see stories acted out in streets, theatres, and inns. As an audience we rarely see the text of the play we are seeing (unless we are studying it): it is aimed chiefly at the actors and technical team who will take the words and convert them into living action on stage.

Before reading

Louis Phillips is an American writer who has written children's stories, journalism, poetry and numerous plays. *Carwash* is a comic sketch with an odd, 'surrealistic' feel (that is, it doesn't seem to follow the expected logic of everyday life).

So: a comedy sketch about a carwash. Make some predictions about who the characters might be and what might happen.

Carwash

Word bank
concerto – piece of classical music for orchestra and one or more soloists
Bermuda Triangle – area of the north-western Atlantic thought by some people to cause aircraft and ships to disappear
lot – parking space: we would probably say forecourt
psychological theory – theory about how people's minds work
put me on the defensive – make me feel it's my fault

(In the dark we hear the sound of a carwash at full throttle. The water hums a powerful spray, the brushes create a concerto of scrub, the vacuum cleaners vacuum, pulling dust and dirt out of some kind of universe. The noise subsides. When the lights come on on the Charm School Carwash, we see a few buckets of soap, large sponges, two or three folding chairs, dirty towels.)

(On stage are two men. **Ken Pfeiffer***, who is dressed in a dark suit and who is carrying a briefcase, and* **Joe Whistler***, a worker at the carwash. Joe is in simple workpants, sneakers, and a white shirt with the name: 'Charm School Carwash'.)*

Pfeiffer: Get me the manager!
Joe: I am the manager.
Pfeiffer: No, you're not the manager. You're a car thief.
Joe: Keep calm.
Pfeiffer: I am calm.
Joe: You're not calm.
Pfeiffer: You're not the manager!
Joe: I am one of the managers. Everyone on the lot is a manager. It's part of a new psychological theory of increasing profits. Make everybody feel the way the owner feels. We learned it from a book about the Japanese.
Pfeiffer: I don't want to hear about the Japanese right now.
Joe: Why? Are they ruining your business too?
Pfeiffer: I don't have a business. And, at the moment, I don't even have a car!
Joe: You have a car. You came in here with a car. You will leave with one.
Pfeiffer: I want to leave with the one I came in.
Joe: You will.
Pfeiffer: Where is it?
Joe: It has to be in there somewhere.
Pfeiffer: It's not in there. I keep telling you. It's not in there. Look!

(*The manager of the carwash enters. She is* **Darlene Silverman.** *In her mid-thirties, she is short, with frizzled hair. She wears a blue jumpsuit.*)

Darlene: What seems to be the trouble here.
Pfeiffer: I want the manager.
Darlene: I am the manager.
Pfeiffer: Of course. Everybody's a manager in this business. It's something you learned from the Japanese...
Darlene: What's that supposed to mean?
Joe: He's upset because he lost his car.
Darlene: He lost his car?
Joe: He lost his car.
Pfeiffer: I lost my car.
Darlene: You lost your car?
Pfeiffer: What are we talking about here?
Joe: I thought we were talking about losing your car.
Pfeiffer: That's right. That's exactly what I'm talking about. Losing my car.
Darlene: If you lost your car, what are you doing at a carwash? It doesn't make any sense to come to a carwash without any car.
Pfeiffer: Are you crazy? What are you talking about? I came here with my car and now I don't have a car. I put it in there. (*Points to the carwash tunnel.*)
Darlene: (*to* **Joe**) What's he talking about?

Joe: He lost his car.
Darlene: He lost his car?
Pfeiffer: I lost my car… in there.
Darlene: Is this some kind of a joke? You lost your car in there?
Pfeiffer: I didn't lose the car. You lost the car.
Darlene: (*to* **Joe**) What's he talking about? It's impossible to lose a car in there.
Pfeiffer: You did something to it.
Joe: I didn't touch the car!
Pfeiffer: Somebody touched the car!
Joe: I don't touch the cars until they come out of the tunnel. Your car didn't come out of the tunnel. Therefore, I didn't touch it.
Darlene: (*to* **Pfeiffer**) See?
Pfeiffer: See what?
Darlene: He didn't touch your car. So what are you complaining about?
Pfeiffer: What am I complaining about?
Darlene: What are you complaining about?
Joe: What's he complaining about?
Pfeiffer: Stop it! I don't want you trying any of your charm school stuff on me.
Joe: What charm school stuff?
Pfeiffer: I don't find any of it charming.
Darlene: I still don't understand what you're complaining about.
Pfeiffer: I told you.
Darlene: You didn't tell me.
Pfeiffer: I drove my car into this Charm School and Carwash…
Darlene: It's not a charm school and carwash. It's Charm School Carwash. It's owned by a woman named Charm School.
Pfeiffer: There's actually a woman named Charm School?
Darlene: Of course there is. You don't think we would actually name a carwash Charm School unless the owner wanted her name upon it. But maybe you think it's funny to make fun of a person's name.
Pfeiffer: Are you the owner?
Darlene: No, I'm the manager.
Joe: One of the managers.
Darlene: My name is Darlene. This is Joe. What's your name?
Pfeiffer: Pfeiffer… Salten Pfeiffer.
Darlene: Salten Pfeiffer and you make fun of someone named Charm School?
Pfeiffer: Don't do this to me!
Darlene: Do what to you?
Pfeiffer: Put me on the defensive. It's you people who are at fault. Not me. I drove my car in here in good faith. Put it on the conveyor belt, got out, came over here, listened to the water, the brushes, and waited for my car to emerge fully cleansed, brand-new as it were…

Joe: And for less than two dollars too. What kind of a bargain is that?
Pfeiffer: But my car didn't come out. What kind of a bargain is that? The $80,000 car wash?
Darlene: $80,000? What kind of car are you driving?
Pfeiffer: It was designed for a movie star.
Darlene: Oh.
Pfeiffer: Oh? What do you mean by 'oh'?
Darlene: I mean you can't expect a movie star's car to act like everybody else's car.
Pfeiffer: I expect it to come out of a carwash.
Darlene: Maybe it's still in there?
Pfeiffer: What is this? The Bermuda Triangle? I bring my car in here and it goes up in a puff of smoke.
Darlene: Smoke? Did you actually see a puff of smoke?
Pfeiffer: I didn't see anything. I have been waiting for my car to come out and it didn't come out.
Darlene: Then why did you say a puff of smoke?
Pfeiffer: It was a figure of speech. A way of talking.
Darlene: Well, don't say it if you don't mean it.
Joe: We looked. It's not in there.
Pfeiffer: I mean it. I just don't believe it. What do you people do? Is it some kind of illusion? Some magician taught you to pluck people's cars out of thin air?
Darlene: How do we know it happened?
Pfeiffer: What do you mean?
Darlene: How do we know you actually came in here with a car?
Pfeiffer: Of course I came in here with a car. What else would I bring to a carwash. My laundry? … That's what I did. I brought you my underwear and called it a Mercedes.
Darlene: No need to talk dirty.
Pfeiffer: I drove in here. I put my Mercedes on the conveyor belt. I got out… The car went through and didn't emerge.
Darlene: You can't prove it. I think you would actually have a difficult time proving you actually brought a car in here.
Pfeiffer: I don't have to prove it!

Louis Philips

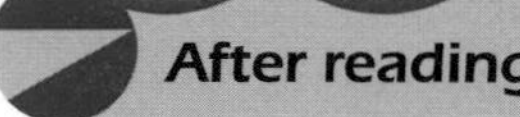

A

1 Look at the first paragraph of stage directions about the setting. Which of these statements is *not* a fair description of the carwash?
   a It is busy.
   b It is working well.
   c It does more than just wash cars.
   d It is completely automatic.
   e It is noisy.

2 What does Joe mean when he says 'everyone on the lot is a manager'?

3 What has happened to Ken Pfeiffer's car?

4 What do we learn in the extract about the kind of car he was driving? Write down two facts about it.

5 How can you tell that the text is written in American English? Try to find several examples.

B

6 'Every character in the play behaves badly.' Do you agree? Explain your answer.

7 The play seems to start in the middle of a conversation – 'Get me the manager!' What effect does this have?

8 The play uses different kinds of humour to make us laugh – funny names, repetition and confusion, jokes, ('What is this? The Bermuda Triangle?'), etc. Write a paragraph about what you find amusing in the extract.

9 How should the text be played on stage – very fast? Seriously? In an exaggerated style? What advice would you give to a cast about to rehearse the play?

1 Imagine Ken Pfeiffer finally storms out of the carwash in disgust, furious that he cannot get sensible answers. Write his letter of complaint to his lawyer in which he explains what has happened.

2 What do you think happens next? Continue the play …

Bernard Shaw: Pygmalion

Before reading

Bernard Shaw is usually recognized as one of the great playwrights of our century, as well as a formidable music-critic and letter-writer. His work has in recent years seemed neglected in English theatres, but *Pygmalion* remains his best-known work. It tells of Professor Higgins, a rude and arrogant language specialist, who takes on the challenge of teaching flower girl Eliza Doolittle to speak in 'proper' English. Like *Educating Rita,* the play raises issues about the damaging effects education can have as well as the benefits.

The extract begins with Higgins' housekeeper, Mrs Pearce, showing Eliza in ...

Do you think people should be taught to give up their local accents and dialects, and learn more standard ones? What are the arguments for and against this?

(Style note: Shaw believed that apostrophes served little useful purpose in most words, so he left them out – as in *arent* and *thats*.)

Word bank

Bell's Visible Speech ... Broad Romic – two ways of copying out speech to show the way it is pronounced
brusquely – briskly and rudely
coaxes – teases
cylinder to use on the phonograph – before tape recorders, wax cylinders were used to record voices. They developed into the records that some people still use on record players
declaiming – speaking loudly, in a wooden manner
deplorable – wretched or sad
exclaiming to the heavens against some feather-weight cross – making a great deal of fuss over nothing
follies – crazy acts
grievance – argument
Lisson Grove lingo – accent from a district of London
pathos – sadness
perplexed – confused
prudery – embarrassment
saucy – cheeky
transcript – written version of the words someone says, like a script
vanity and consequential air – self-importance
yə-oo – Shaw uses the 'schwa' – ə – to indicate the most frequently-used sound in English. It's the 'e' sound in 'the'

Pygmalion

Mrs Pearce: (*hesitating, evidently perplexed*) A young woman asks to see you, sir.

Higgins: A young woman! What does she want?

Mrs Pearce: Well, sir, she says youll be glad to see her when you know what she's come about. She's quite a common girl, sir. Very common indeed. I should have sent her away, only I thought perhaps you wanted her to talk into your machines. I hope Ive not done wrong; but really you see such queer people sometimes – youll excuse me, I'm sure, sir –

Higgins: Oh, thats all right, Mrs Pearce. Has she an interesting accent?

Mrs Pearce: Oh, something dreadful, sir, really. I dont know how you can take an interest in it.

Higgins: (*to* **Pickering**) Lets have her up. Shew her up, Mrs Pearce. (*He rushes across to his working table and picks out a cylinder to use on the phonograph.*)

Mrs Pearce: (*only half resigned to it*) Very well, sir. It's for you to say. (*She goes downstairs.*)

Higgins: This is rather a bit of luck. I'll shew you how I make records. We'll set her talking; and I'll take it down first in Bell's Visible Speech; then in broad Romic; and then we'll get her on the phonograph so that you can turn her on as often as you like with the written transcript before you.

Mrs Pearce: (*returning*) This is the young woman, sir.

(*The* **flower girl** *enters in state. She has a hat with three ostrich feathers, orange, sky-blue, and red. She has a nearly clean apron and the shoddy coat has been tidied a little. The pathos of this deplorable figure, with its innocent vanity and consequential air, touches* **Pickering**, *who has already straightened himself in the presence of* **Mrs Pearce**. *But as to* **Higgins**, *the only distinction he makes between men and women is that when he is neither bullying not exclaiming to the heavens against some feather-weight cross, he coaxes women as a child coaxes its nurse when it wants to get anything out of her.*)

Higgins: (*brusquely, recognizing her with unconcealed disappointment, and at once, babylike, making an intolerable grievance of it*) Why, this is the girl I jotted down last night. She's no use; I've got all the records I want of the Lisson Grove lingo; and I'm not going to waste another cylinder on it. (*To the girl*) Be off with you: I don't want you.

The Flower Girl: Dont you be so saucy. You aint heard what I come for yet. (*To* **Mrs Pearce**, *who is waiting at the door for further instructions*) Did you tell him I come in a taxi?

Mrs Pearce: Nonsense, girl! What do you think a gentleman like Mr Higgins cares what you came in?

The Flower Girl: Oh, we are proud! He aint above giving lessons, not him: I heard him say so. Well, I aint come here to ask for any compliment; and if my money's not good enough I can go elsewhere.

Higgins: Good enough for what?

The Flower Girl: Good enough for yə-oo. Now you know, dont you? I'm come to have lessons, I am. And to pay for em tə-oo: make no mistake.

Higgins: (*stupent*) Well!!! (*Recovering his breath with a gasp*) What do you expect me to say to you?

The Flower Girl: Well, if you was a gentleman, you might ask me to sit down, I think. Dont I tell you I'm bringing you business?

Higgins: Pickering: shall we ask this baggage to sit down, or shall we throw her out of the window?

The Flower Girl: (*running away in terror to the piano, where she turns at bay*) Ah-ah-oh-ow-ow-ow-oo! (*Wounded and whimpering*) I wont be called a baggage when Ive offered to pay like any lady.

(*Motionless, the two men stare at her from the other side of the room, amazed.*)

Pickering: (*Gently*) But what is it you want?

The Flower Girl: I want to be a lady in a flower shop stead of selling at the corner of Tottenham Court Road. But they wont take me unless I can talk more genteel. He said he could teach me. Well, here I am ready to pay him – not asking any favour – and he treats me zif I was dirt.

Mrs Pearce: How can you be such a foolish ignorant girl as to think you could afford to pay Mr Higgins?

The Flower Girl: Why shouldnt I? I know what lessons cost as well as you do; and I'm ready to pay.

Higgins: How much?

The Flower Girl: (*coming back to him, triumphant*) Now youre talking! I thought youd come off it when you saw a chance of getting back a bit of what you chucked at me last night. (*Confidentially*) Youd had a drop in, hadnt you?

Higgins: (*peremptorily*) Sit down.

The Flower Girl: Oh, if youre going to make a compliment of it –

Higgins: (*thundering at her*) Sit down.

Mrs Pearce: (*severely*) Sit down, girl. Do as youre told.

The Flower Girl: Ah-ah-ah-ow-ow-oo. (*She stands, half rebellious, half bewildered.*)

Pickering: (*very courteous*) Wont you sit down? (*He places the stray chair near the hearthrug between himself and* **Higgins**.)

The Flower Girl: (*coyly*) Dont mind if I do. (*She sits down.* **Pickering** *returns to the hearthrug.*)

Higgins: Whats your name?
The Flower Girl: Liza Doolittle.
Higgins: (*declaiming gravely*) Eliza, Elizabeth, Betsy and Bess,
They went to the woods to get a bird's nes':
Pickering: They found a nest with four eggs in it:
Higgins: They took one apiece, and left three in it.

(*They laugh heartily at their own fun.*)

Liza: Oh, dont be silly.
Mrs Pearce: (*placing herself behind* **Liza's** *chair*) You mustnt speak to the gentleman like that.
Liza: Well, why wont he speak sensible to me?
Higgins: Come back to business. How much do you propose to pay me for the lessons?
Liza: Oh, I know whats right. A lady friend of mine gets French lessons for eighteenpence an hour from a real French gentleman. Well, you wouldnt have the face to ask me the same for teaching me my own language as you would for French; so I wont give more than a shilling. Take it or leave it.
Higgins: (*walking up and down the room, rattling his keys and his cash in his pockets*) You know, Pickering, if you consider a shilling, not as a simple shilling, but as a percentage of this girl's income, it works out as fully equivalent to sixty or seventy guineas from a millionaire.
Pickering: How so?
Higgins: Figure it out. A millionaire has about £150 a day. She earns about half-a-crown.
Liza: (*haughtily*) Who told you I only –
Higgins: (*continuing*) She offers me two-fifths of her day's income for a lesson. Two-fifths of a millionaire's income for a day would be somewhere about £60. It's handsome. By George, it's enormous! It's the biggest offer I ever had.
Liza: (*rising, terrified*) Sixty pounds! What are you talking about? I never offered you sixty pounds.
Where would I get –
Higgins: Hold your tongue.
Liza: (*weeping*) But I aint got sixty pounds. Oh –
Mrs Pearce: Dont cry, you silly girl. Sit down. Nobody is going to touch your money.
Higgins: Somebody is going to touch you, with a broomstick, if you dont stop snivelling. Sit down.
Liza: (*obeying slowly*) Ah-ah-ah-ow-oo-o! One would think you was my father.

Higgins: If I decide to teach you, I'll be worse than two fathers to you. Here. (*He offers her his silk handkerchief.*)

Liza: Whats this for?

Higgins: To wipe your eyes. To wipe any part of your face that feels moist. Remember: thats your handkerchief; and thats your sleeve. Dont mistake the one for the other if you wish to become a lady in a shop.

(**Liza**, *utterly bewildered, stares helplessly at him.*)

Mrs Pearce: It's no use talking to her like that, Mr Higgins: she doesn't understand you. Besides, youre quite wrong: she doesnt do it that way at all. (*She takes the handkerchief.*)

Liza: (*snatching it*) Here! You give me that handkerchief. He gev it to me, not to you.

Pickering: (*laughing*) He did. I think it must be regarded as her property, Mrs Pearce.

Mrs Pearce: (*resigning herself*) Serve you right, Mr Higgins.

Pickering: Higgins: I'm interested. What about the ambassador's garden party? I'll say youre the greatest teacher alive if you make that good. I'll bet you all the expenses of the experiment you cant do it. And I'll pay for the lessons.

Liza: Oh, you are real good. Thank you, Captain.

Higgins: (*tempted, looking at her*) It's almost irresistible. She's so deliciously low – so horribly dirty –

Liza: (*protesting extremely*) Ah-ah-ah-ah-ow-ow-oo-oo!!! I aint dirty: I washed my face and hands afore I come, I did.

Pickering: Youre certainly not going to turn her head with flattery, Higgins.

Mrs Pearce: (*uneasy*) Oh, dont say that, sir: theres more ways than one of turning a girl's head; and nobody can do it better than Mr Higgins, though he may not always mean it. I do hope, sir, you wont encourage him to do anything foolish.

Higgins: (*becoming excited as the idea grows on him*) What is life but a series of inspired follies? The difficulty is to find them to do. Never lose a chance: it doesnt come every day. I shall make a duchess of this draggletailed guttersnipe.

Liza: (*strongly deprecating this view of her*) Ah-ah-ah-ow-ow-oo!

Higgins: (*carried away*) Yes: in six months – in three if she has a good ear and a quick tongue – I'll take her anywhere and pass her off as anything. We'll start today: now! this moment! Take her away and clean her, Mrs Pearce. Monkey Brand, if it wont come off any other way. Is there a good fire in the kitchen?

Mrs Pearce: (*protesting*) Yes; but –

Higgins: (*storming on*) Take all her clothes off and burn them. Ring up Whitely or somebody for new ones. Wrap her up in brown paper til they come.

Liza: Youre no gentleman, youre not, to talk of such things. I'm a good girl, I am; and I know what the like of you are, I do.

Higgins: We want none of your Lisson Grove prudery here, young woman. Youve got to learn to behave like a duchess. Take her away, Mrs Pearce. If she gives you any trouble, wallop her.

Liza: (*springing up and running between* **Pickering** *and* **Mrs Pearce** *for protection*) No! I'll call the police, I will.

Mrs Pearce: But Ive no place to put her.

Higgins: Put her in the dustbin.

Liza: Ah-ah-ah-ow-ow-oo!

Pickering: Oh come, Higgins! Be reasonable.

Mrs Pearce: (*resolutely*) You must be reasonable, Mr Higgins: really you must. You cant walk over everybody like this.

Bernard Shaw

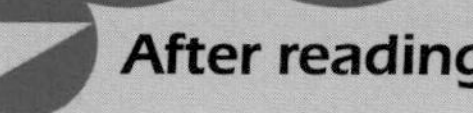

After reading

A

1 What are your first impressions of Higgins and Liza? Make a note of them in a table like this:

Higgins	Liza

2 What do you make of Mrs Pearce's attitude to Professor Higgins – tolerant, likes him, irritated by him, neutral? Choose a word which you think is most appropriate (either from the list above, or your own choice) and write a sentence explaining your decision.

3 How does Professor Higgins already know Liza?

4 Near the start of the extract, Higgins says to Liza, 'Be off with you'. By the end he is saying that he will 'make a duchess' of her. Explain why he changes his mind.

B

5 Professor Higgins is extremely rude. Do you think we are supposed to like or dislike him? Try to explain why.

6 What overall impressions do you form of Liza? How much do you sympathize with her and how much does she annoy you? Write a paragraph explaining your feelings about her.

7 Many people have been irritated by the treatment of women in this play. What examples of sexism can you find?

8 After the way she is treated, do you think Liza is right to accept the speech lessons, or should she walk out? Explain why.

1 Imagine Liza Doolittle's diary that evening. What would she say about her visit to Professor Higgins' house? Have a go at writing it. You might even try to imitate Liza's dialect in what she writes.

2 Professor Higgins changes his mind about Liza in the short space of this extract. Interview him about his first impressions of her, and why he then saw her as an interesting language challenge. Try to show what Higgins' character is like – his rudeness, for example, and the way he shows off. You might begin like this:

Interviewer: What was your first impression when Mrs Pearce showed Eliza Doolittle into your study?

Higgins: I thought, 'Oh no', not her again …

POETRY

Reading and responding to poetry

This section contains a range of poetry, including:
- poems from this century and poems from the past
- poems from a variety of cultures (for example, the USA, the Caribbean, Africa, Britain)
- poems that are easy to follow
- poems that need untangling.

Some students worry about reading poems. Look at these comments from a Year 8 group:

'Everyone else seems to understand poetry. Sometimes I can't make sense of it.'
'I really like poetry – but reading it and answering questions on it spoils it.'
'I like poetry that rhymes. If it doesn't rhyme, it doesn't seem like proper poetry.'

Perhaps more than any other kind of text, poetry needs close reading, so in this section you will get opportunity to develop these skills:

Key skills

- Becoming more confident in reading a range of styles of poems.
- Looking at what the poems are about.
- Looking at the way the writers use language.
- Comparing poems.

Vicki Feaver: Slow Reader

Before reading

Some people hate school and seem to get very little out of it. Do you think they should be forced to sit through lessons, or should they be allowed to do other activities? Should young people have more right to choose? Or would they be at a disadvantage if they did not have a full education?

Word bank
colt – young horse
impassable – cannot be crossed
shying – pulling away from
solemn – serious

Slow Reader

He can make sculptures
And fabulous machines
Invent games, tell jokes
Give solemn, adult advice
But he is slow to read.
When I take him on my knee
With his *Ladybird* book
He gazes into the air
Sighing and shaking his head
Like an old man
Who knows the mountains
Are impassable.

He toys with words
Letting them grow cold
As gristly meat
Until I relent
And let him wriggle free –
A fish returning
To its element
Or a white-eyed colt
Shying from the bit
As if he sees
That if he takes it
In his mouth
He'll never run
Quite free again.

Vicki Feaver

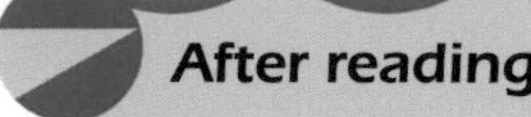

After reading

A

1 List four things the writer admires about the boy.
2 Does the writer feel frustrated that he does not read, or can she understand why he is reluctant? Explain your answer.
3 What do you think the writer means in these lines?:
  a 'He toys with words
  Letting them grow cold
  As gristly meat'
  b 'A fish returning to its element'
  c 'He'll never run
  Quite free again'
4 In what ways does the boy seem grown up?

B

5 Look at this comment that one student made after reading the poem:
  'When I saw the title, I thought this poem would be about someone who couldn't read very well. It's actually about someone who doesn't *want* to read.'
  Do you agree? Write a brief paragraph agreeing or disagreeing with this statement. Support your viewpoint with quotations from the poem.
6 How does the writer make us feel sympathetic towards the boy?
7 Do you think the boy should be forced to go to school? Wouldn't he be better following his own interests? Write a brief paragraph explaining your point of view.

Extended assignments

1 Imagine you are the child in the poem. Write about your attitude to reading: how you feel about sitting reading *Ladybird* books; what you have achieved without being able to read; why you feel learning to read might actually limit you.
2 In response to the poem, put the case *for* reading. What do you remember about your own experiences of learning to read? Who read to you? Which books do you especially remember? What did you enjoy or dislike about this early process of being read to? What do you recall of infant and junior school – reading schemes, flash cards, different books? How did your reading develop … and so on?
  Try to write your own personal reading history from your early years up to around the age of 11.

Rudyard Kipling: The Way Through the Woods

Before reading

Rudyard Kipling is perhaps best known for his collection of stories, *The Jungle Book*. The Disney film version is based on them. He was also a highly-popular poet until the First World War, when he fell out of fashion. Even so, in a recent BBC survey of Britain's favourite poem, the winner was a Kipling poem, 'If–'.

Look at the title of this poem. Do you think it will be:

- a poem about a journey?
- a description of nature?
- a ghostly tale?
- a description of a special place in a forest?
- a story told as a poem?

Word bank
anemones – woodland flowers
broods – sits
coppice – small wood
solitudes – lonely atmosphere

The Way Through the Woods

They shut the road through the woods
Seventy years ago.
Weather and rain have undone it again,
And now you would never know
There was once a road through the woods
Before they planted the trees.
It is underneath the coppice and heath
And the thin anemones.
Only the keeper sees
That, where the ring-dove broods,
And the badgers roll at ease,
There was once a road through the woods.

Yet, if you enter the woods
Of a summer evening late,
When the night-air cools on the trout-ringed pools
Where the otter whistles his mate,
(They fear not men in the woods,
Because they see so few.)
You will hear the beat of a horse's feet,
And the swish of a skirt in the dew,
Steadily cantering through
The misty solitudes,
As though they perfectly knew
The old lost road through the woods...
But there is no road through the woods.

Rudyard Kipling

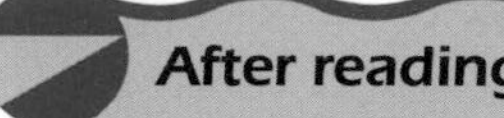

After reading

A

1. How long ago did they shut the road?
2. What did people do to cover up the road?
3. What do you think the writer means when he says, 'Weather and rain have undone it again' (line 3)?
4. Why are the otters in the woods not shy of human beings?
5. Choose a line which shows that nature has now taken over the space where the road used to be.

B

6. Why do you think they shut the road in the first place?
7. Who might the people have been who the writer describes in the last part of the poem?
8. How do you explain the last seven lines of the poem?
9. In some ways the text reads like a story. What makes it feel like a poem?
10. What do you like or dislike about the poem?

Extended assignments

1. Use the poem as the starting-point for a mysterious tale. Imagine you are out walking alone and find yourself in these woods. You notice how strangely deserted they seem, as if human beings never set foot in them. You notice wildlife, but no hint even of people. And then you hear the ghostly echo of voices and horses' hooves… What happens next?
2. Explore the poem further by writing another verse, which develops the idea of who the people in the woods might be. Try to make your new verse sound as close as possible to the old one. Then write a paragraph commenting on what you have written, the language decisions you made, and how well you think the poem works.

Advice panel: writing about poetry

Remember that reading poetry takes time because in a poem, language is usually concentrated. We need to take time unpacking it. Try to:

- look at the title and predict what the poem will be about
- read it aloud or in your head so that you can 'hear' the rhythms and rhymes
- make notes as you read
- expect to read it at least three times before writing about it
- remember that we're not interested in right answers – there's no such thing. We want to know what you notice about the poem.

Jack Mapanje: The Sweet Brew at Chitakale

Before reading

This poem from Africa describes in simple language a brief moment of distress and also strength in an old woman's life.

When someone treats you with cruelty, how do you tend to react – with patience, putting up with their action, or by lashing out at them? Watch the way the old woman responds.

Word bank
deposited – placed
exchange – purchase (they are exchanging money for a drink)
gourdful – large hollow nut-shell containing the drink
thobwa – a sweet drink brewed from millet

The Sweet Brew at Chitakale

The old woman squats before a clay jar of thobwa
She uncovers the basket lid from the jar and
Stirs attention with a gourdful of the brew.

The customers have all been here: cyclists
In dripping sweat have deposited their coins
In the basket gulping down their share.

Pedestrians on various chores have talked
Before the exchange and then cooled their
Parched throats to their money's worth,

But this bus passenger bellows for a gourdful
From the window, drinks deliberately slowly until
The conductor presses the go-button –

The woman picks up the pieces of her broken
Gourd, and dusting her bottom, again squats
Confronting her brew with a borrowed cup.

Jack Mapanje

After reading

A

1 What do you think the writer means when he says that the woman 'stirs attention' with her brew?
2 Which word tells you that the cyclists are thirsty?
3 Which of these words best describes the bus passenger?

rude ignorant loud thirsty pushy selfish unkind

Write down the word and then write a sentence explaining why you chose it.
4 Why do you think the passenger drinks 'deliberately slowly'?
5 What does the old woman do at the end of the poem, after her gourd has been smashed?

B

6 How do you feel about the woman's reaction? Do you respect her response, or should she have behaved differently? Explain your ideas.

Extended assignments

1 Imagine you are a passer-by – perhaps one of the cyclists or pedestrians in the market square. Describe the event from your point of view. You might mention: your impression of the scene; your first sighting of the old woman; your drink of thobwa; your first impression of the bus passenger; what happened next and how people reacted.
2 Write a response to the poem in which you comment upon:
- the storyline
- the character of the old woman
- the character of the bus passenger
- the way the poet creates a sense of setting
- the poet's choice of language.

Conclude by writing about what you like and dislike about the poem.

Poetry Comparison 1: Judith Wright and Anne Stevenson

Advice panel: comparing poems

Some people find comparing poems easier and more interesting than just looking at one poem on its own. They feel it gives them more to say. Some points to look out for:

1. How do the poems look different on the page?
2. How is their subject-matter different?
3. What are the similarities and differences in the writers' feelings and attitudes?
4. How does the language compare – which is simpler, more descriptive, more emotional, more personal, more rhythmic …?

Before reading

These two poems are concerned with the way humans treat the environment – the rainforests and the coast.

What do you predict the writers will say about the way humans treat nature?

Rainforest

Word bank

begonia beds – lines of bright flowers
distinguish – sort out one thing from another
ornamental – purely for decoration

The forest drips and glows with green.
The tree-frog croaks his far-off song.
His voice is stillness, moss and rain
drunk from the forest ages long.

We cannot understand that call
unless we move into his dream,
where all is one and one is all
and frog and python are the same.

We with our quick dividing eyes
measure, distinguish and are gone.
The forest burns, the tree-frog dies,
yet one is all and all are one.

Judith Wright

The Fish are all Sick

The fish are all sick, the great whales dead,
The villages stranded in stone on the coast,
Ornamental, like pearls on the fringe of a coat.
Sea men, who knew what the ocean did,
Turned their low houses away from the surf.
But new men who come to be rural and safe
Add big glass views and begonia beds.
Water keeps to itself.
White lip after lip
Curls to a close on the littered beach.
Something is sicker and blacker than fish.
And closing its grip, and closing its grip.

Anne Stevenson

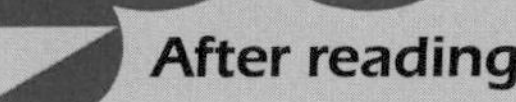

After reading

A: Rainforest

1 What picture do you get in your mind when the writer says, 'The forest drips and glows with green'?
2 In the first verse the writer describes a frog. Do you think she likes it or is afraid of it? How can you tell?
3 What impression of human beings does she give when she writes:
'We with our quick dividing eyes
measure, distinguish and are gone'?
4 What do you think the last two lines of the poem might be saying?

A: The Fish are all Sick

5 Who lives by the sea now?

6 What has killed the fish and the whales?

7 What do you think the writer means when she writes:
'White lip after lip
Curls to a close on the littered beach'?

8 The writer warns us about something that is 'sicker and blacker than fish'. What do you think she might mean?

B: Comparisons

9 If you had to sum up in one sentence what each poem is about, what would you say? Try to write a clear sentence for each poem.

10 Compare the way human beings are portrayed in the two poems – is it completely negative?

11 Anne Stevenson's poem is much more angry in tone than Judith Wright's. Compare the emotional mood in the two poems. How do the poets show their own feelings?

1 Using Anne Stevenson's poem, write a speech aimed at the new coastal dwellers, to show them the damage they are doing and the worrying trouble that is building up for the future. Address the speech directly to the people who have moved to the houses with 'big glass views and begonia beds'. You might mention:
- who used to live here
- why they have left
- what is happening to the sea life
- what might happen in the future
- what people should do to improve the situation.

2 Using the notes you have made in the earlier questions, write a comparison of the two poems – what they are about, the way they are written, their authors' attitudes. Conclude by saying which you like best.

Thomas Hood: I Remember, I Remember

Before reading

Thomas Hood was a popular poet in the first half of the nineteenth century. He was particularly famous for his ballads – poems which told stories of ordinary people, often with tragic endings. This poem is different. It is a kind of autobiography, in which the poet thinks back to his youth.

Give yourself thirty seconds of concentrated silence. What are the key memories – good and bad – that flood into your mind in that time? Some people remember childhood as a time of sunshine and laughter. Is that because our memories weed out the bad bits?

Word bank
ignorance – lack of knowledge
laburnum – a tree of bright yellow flowers

I Remember, I Remember

I remember, I remember,
The house where I was born,
The little window where the sun
Came peeping in at morn;
He never came a wink too soon,
Nor brought too long a day,
But now, I often wish the night
Had borne my breath away!

I remember, I remember,
The roses, red and white,
The violets, and the lily-cups,
Those flowers made of light!
The lilacs where the robin built,
And where my brother set
The laburnum on his birthday, –
The tree is living yet!

I remember, I remember,
Where I used to swing,
And thought the air must rush as fresh
To swallows on the wing;
My spirit flew in feathers then,
That is so heavy now,
And summer pools could hardly cool
The fever on my brow!

I remember, I remember,
The fir trees dark and high;
I used to think their slender tops
Were close against the sky:
It was a childish ignorance,
But now 'tis little joy
To know I'm farther off from heaven
Than when I was a boy.

Thomas Hood

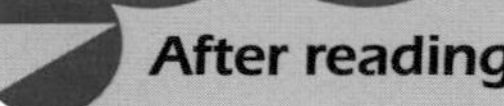

After reading

A

1 Thomas Hood's chief memories from childhood come from nature. Write down three specific objects he remembers.

2 In the first verse, how does the writer make the sun seem friendly?

3 Why is the laburnum tree in verse 2 particularly special to Thomas Hood?

B

4 The writer remembers the joys of childhood. But he also hints that he is not so happy now. Find a quotation to support this.

5 Write about the way the writer seems to have changed in his later life.

6 Some readers have said that this isn't a poem about childhood. It's about growing up. Do you agree? Say why.

7 How does Thomas Hood use language to make his childhood memories seem attractive? For example, look at the way he describes the sun; the way nature is presented; the impression you get of his relationship with his brother. Does Hood make it all seem a little *too* perfect?

Extended assignments

1 Using your answers to the questions above, write a commentary on Thomas Hood's poem. Write about each verse in turn, looking at:

- what he describes
- the feelings he has
- the impressions we get of the narrator
- the language he uses (vocabulary, rhythm, rhyme).

Finish by writing about what you particularly like or dislike about the poem.

2 Imagine Thomas Hood was writing about his childhood memories in prose rather than verse. How would the poem feel different if it had been written as a straight piece of autobiographical writing? Have a go at writing two or three paragraphs, based on the memories in the poem. You might begin:

> 'I remember the house I was born in. It had a small window where the sun streamed in each morning ...'

Then write a paragraph explaining the changes you made, and how the prose version of the text feels different.

Philip Larkin: The North Ship

Before reading

Philip Larkin's poem is sub-titled 'Legend'. A legend is a tale which may be true, or may not, such as the story of Robin Hood.

What ingredients do we normally expect to find in a legend? Read this list and decide which are the three key ingredients:

- the main character should be someone we like or admire
- the basic story is an adventure
- the heroine or hero helps other people and possibly saves their lives
- there are wicked characters
- magic is usually involved
- the story takes place either in the past or the future
- there is always a happy ending.

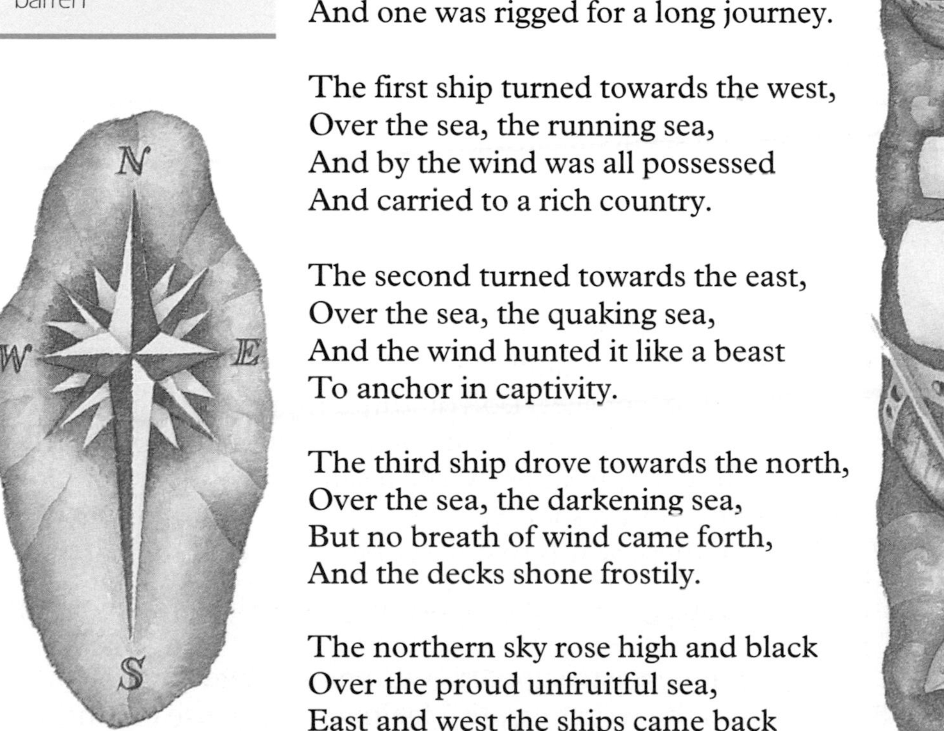

The North Ship

Legend

I saw three ships go sailing by,
Over the sea, the lifting sea,
And the wind rose in the morning sky,
And one was rigged for a long journey.

The first ship turned towards the west,
Over the sea, the running sea,
And by the wind was all possessed
And carried to a rich country.

The second turned towards the east,
Over the sea, the quaking sea,
And the wind hunted it like a beast
To anchor in captivity.

The third ship drove towards the north,
Over the sea, the darkening sea,
But no breath of wind came forth,
And the decks shone frostily.

The northern sky rose high and black
Over the proud unfruitful sea,
East and west the ships came back
Happily or unhappily:

Word bank
captivity – imprisonment
unfruitful – infertile, barren

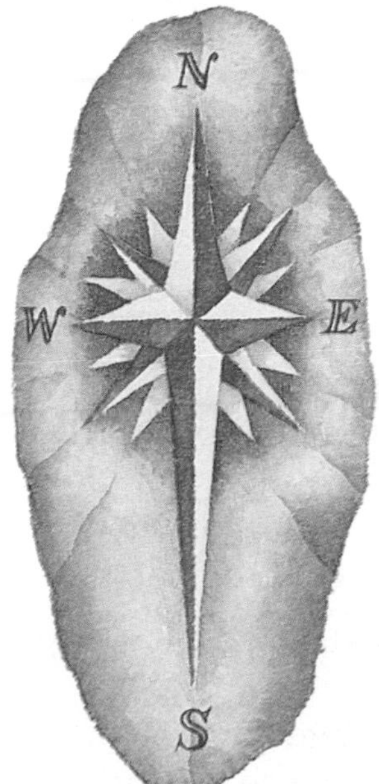

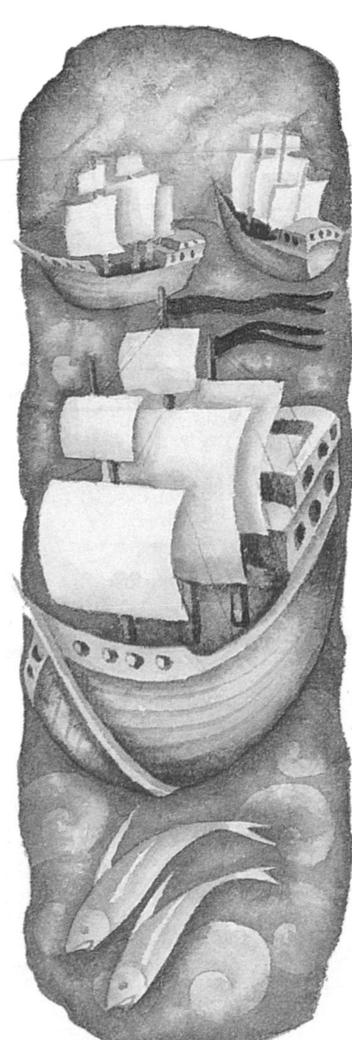

But the third went wide and far
Into an unforgiving sea
Under a fire-spilling star,
And it was rigged for a long journey.

Philip Larkin

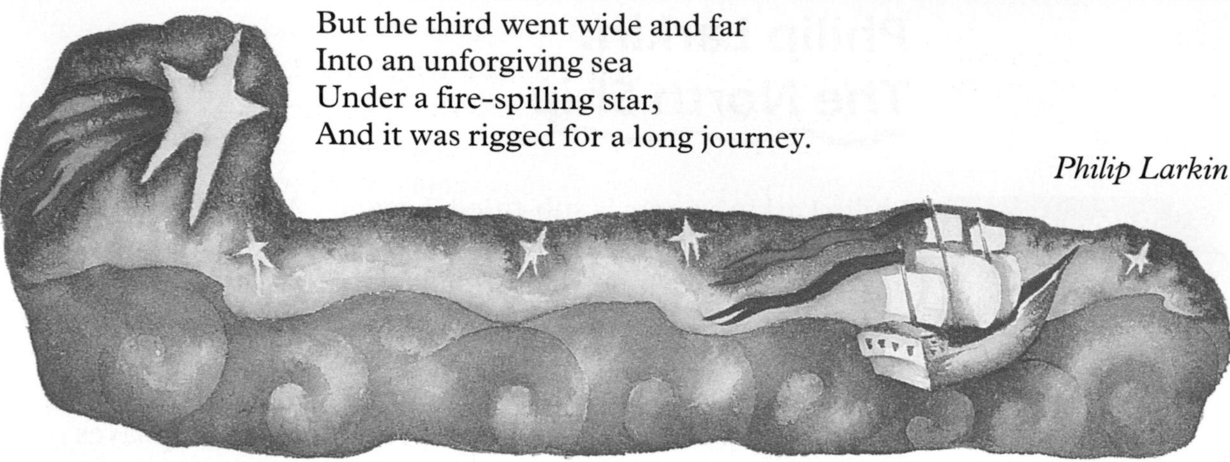

After reading

A

1 The second line mentions 'the lifting sea'. What do you think this might mean?

2 Use this table to describe what we learn about each of the ships – what it is like, where it is going, what happens to it.

Ship 1	Ship 2	Ship 3

3 What do you think will happen to the third ship?

4 In the third verse the writer describes the wind. How does he make it seem menacing?

B

5 What picture do you get in your mind of the 'fire-spilling star' in the last verse?

6 Philip Larkin's poem echoes the Christmas carol, 'I Saw Three Ships Come Sailing In', except that his ships are all setting off on voyages. Do you think that each ship might stand for something – a belief, or an emotion, for example? Or are they simply ships? Write a sentence or two explaining your response.

7 Which of these words best describes the feel of the poem?

lively exciting cheerful worrying pessimistic hopeful

Write a sentence to support your point of view.

8 How does the writer create a feeling of suspense or tension in the poem?

1 Imagine you are at the dock watching the three ships set off on their different journeys. Describe the atmosphere; the mood of the crew on each ship; the behaviour of the observers on land. Try to create a vivid piece of descriptive writing.

2 Write a sequel to Philip Larkin's poem, about the voyage of the North Ship – where it goes and what it does. Does it ever return? Try to write it in the form Larkin has used – six verses of four lines each, with similar rhythm and rhyme. You will need to redraft your work to get it to a final form you are happy with.

Advice panel: looking at rhyme schemes

Sometimes you are invited to write another verse or section of a poem. This is a good way of assessing how much you understood the style as well as the content of the text.

It is important to look at the writer's rhyme scheme – the way the rhymes in the poem are organized. When studying poetry, we normally label each line with a letter. If one line rhymes with another, then it shares the same letter – like this:

I saw three ships go sailing by, (A)
Over the sea, the lifting sea, (B)
And the wind rose in the morning sky, (A)
And one was rigged for a long journey. (B)

The words that rhyme – by/sky and sea/journey – are linked by the same letter. This is a good technique to use when looking at the way a poem is organized. Labelling the poet's existing lines in this way will also give you a good starting-point when writing your own verse in the style of another poem.

Carole Satyamurti: Day Trip

Before reading

Most people love going to the seaside. In Carole Satyamurti's poem two elderly ladies take a day-trip to the Essex coast. For them, paddling in the sea is particularly special ...

Do you enjoy walking in the sea? Before you read the poem, think about what it feels like to do this.

Do you think you will feel the same when you are old?

Word bank
hems – the stitched edge of clothes, curtains, etc.
splayed – wide apart

Day Trip

Two women, seventies, hold hands
on the edge of Essex,
hair in strong nets,
shrieked laughter echoing gulls
as shingle sucks from under feet
easing in brine.

There must be an unspoken point
when the sea feels like
their future. No longer paddling,
ankles submerge in lace,
in satin ripple.
Dress hems darken.

They do not risk their balance
for the shimmering of ships
at the horizon's sweep
as, thigh deep, they inch on
fingers splayed, wrists bent,
learning to walk again.

Carole Satyamurti

After reading

A

1 How can you tell that the women are enjoying being in the sea?

2 Why do you think the women have their 'hair in strong nets'? What does this detail tell us about them, as well as about the weather?

3 What do you think the writer means when she says their feet are 'easing in brine'?
4 At the end of verse 2, 'Dress hems darken'. Why?
5 What do you think the writer means when she describes the women as 'learning to walk again'?

B

6 Try to explain, in your own words, what the writer means when she says:
'There must be an unspoken point
when the sea feels like
their future.'
7 This poem doesn't appear to have many of the features we expect from poetry. It doesn't rhyme. It has no definite rhythm. What, for you, makes it a poem?
8 For some readers the sea is a reminder of death. Others think of birth. Do you think that this poem could be seen as about more than a simple trip to the seaside? Try to explain your response in a sentence or two.

Extended assignments

1 The women's day-trip has meant a great deal to them. Why has it been so special? Imagine the letter one of them might write to the other a few months later, looking back on their glorious day trip. She might relive the atmosphere, the feeling of the soothing sea on her legs, the memories it brought back, her thoughts about the future. You might start your letter:

> 'Dear Elsie,
> Remember that hot July day we spent in Frinton ...?

2 Imagine a poem which described two tiny children taking their first steps into the sea. How would the mood and emotions be different? Experiment with your own poem, using this theme. Try to capture the children's excitement and joy at being in the sea, and also their delight in being with each other. Alternatively, you might imagine the children are a little afraid of this new experience.

The two children could even be the two old ladies, around seventy years ago.

Then write a paragraph saying what you are happy with and unhappy with in your poem, and highlighting the problems you faced.

Derek Walcott: Dark August

Before reading

Some people believe that we prefer the seasons we were born in – so a summer child always likes the summer best. What is your favourite season of the year, and what, in particular, do you feel about August? (End of summer? Blackberry-picking? Return to school haunts you?)

This poem from the Caribbean uses a technique called *personification* to focus on the month of August, and the summer sun. If you had to give the sun a character, how would you describe it? What would it be like and how would it behave?

Dark August

Word bank
broods – stays, thinking about something else
emerge – appear

So much rain, so much life like the swollen sky
of this black August. My sister, the sun,
broods in her yellow room and won't come out.

Everything goes to hell; the mountains fume
like a kettle, rivers over-run, still,
she will not rise and turn off the rain.

She's in her room, fondling old things,
my poems, turning her album. Even if thunder falls
like a crash of plates from the sky,

she does not come out.
Don't you know I love you but am hopeless
at fixing the rain? But I am learning slowly

to love the dark days, the steaming hills,
the air with gossiping mosquitoes,
and to sip the medicine of bitterness,

so that when you emerge, my sister,
parting the beads of the rain,
with your forehead of flowers and eyes of forgiveness,

all will not be as it was, but it will be true,
(you see they will not let me love
as I want), because my sister, then

I would have learnt to love black days like bright ones,
the black rain, the white hills, when once
I loved only my happiness and you.

Derek Walcott

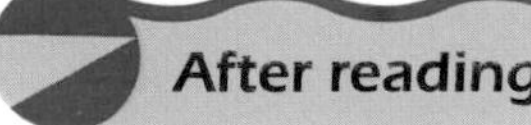

After reading

A

1 This poem is difficult to follow at first. Which of these statements seems to be the best description of what it is about?
  - **a** The narrator hates the rainy days and wishes the sun would return.
  - **b** The narrator tries to persuade his sister, the sun, to bring sunshine into the world.
  - **c** The narrator hopes that his sister the sun will return soon but, in the meantime, finds that he enjoys the darker weather.
  - **d** It is a love poem to the sun.

2 In the first line the writer describes the sky as 'swollen'. What picture does this create in your mind?

3 In the second verse the writer says that the 'mountains fume like a kettle'. What picture do you see?

B

4 The writer uses a technique called *personification* – describing the sun and rain as if they were people. What kind of person is the sun?

5 How does the narrator's attitude to the rain change during the poem?

6 If you didn't know that this poem was set in the Caribbean, would you be able to tell from the text itself? Can you find any clues about its setting?

7 The vocabulary of the poem is mostly straightforward. Yet the poem as a whole isn't easy to follow at first. Try to describe what it is about the poem which makes it difficult.

8 If you wrote the text out as if it was a story, so that it no longer looked like a poem on the page, what difference would it make? Would you be able to tell that this was a poem? Write a paragraph about the language of the text and, in particular, the features which clearly identify it as poetry. You might refer to:
  - rhythm
  - rhyme
  - images
  - comparisons (similes and metaphors)
  - repetitions of sounds and words
  - other patterns you notice.

Extended assignments

1 Use the poem as the opening for a piece of creative writing. It is another day of dark, unending rain and no hint of sunshine. What happens?

2 Write the sun's reply, either in verse or prose. Sitting in her yellow room, listening to the whining of her brother, how does she reply?

Olga Benjamin: Flood

Before reading

Olga Benjamin's poem is about a relationship between a man and woman and the way it changes over the years. Many relationships have one partner who is more dominant – who makes many of the decisions and keeps things moving.

As you read 'Flood', look carefully to see who you think is the dominant partner.

Flood

Word bank

arteries – thick pipes inside our bodies which carry the blood from our hearts
constricted – tightened
Jerez – a Spanish town, famous for making sherry
Seville – a port in southern Spain

My father's temper was as hot
as Seville in August, black
as a bull's hide, harsh
as Jerez leather.

What little heat remains
runs in arteries
constricted as Lancashire canals.

My mother was moderate, calm,
white-skinned, fair.
She went dancing in the 1920's,
asked permission to cut her hair.

Now, she has to rely on tears,
and even they fall
too frequently
to count.

I think she weeps to keep my father flowing,
and he, knowing,
watches the flood
that will take them both
down.

Olga Benjamin

After reading

A

1 The first verse describes what the writer's father used to be like. Write down two things we learn about him.

2 The second verse describes what the father is like now. Write down two things we learn.

3 In what ways was the mother different from the father?

4 Why do you think she used to ask 'permission to cut her hair'?

5 What do you think the writer means when she says, 'Now, she has to rely on tears'?

B

6 Say, in your own words, what you think the final verse means.

7 Who do you think is the more powerful partner in the marriage? Explain your answer carefully.

8 Why do you think the poem is called 'Flood'?

Extended assignments

1 The poem describes the way a marriage develops over the years. Using the clues in the poem, write about the couple – what they were both like in their youth, their similarities and differences, how they have changed, how they behave towards one another, and hints about their future.

2 The poem hints at the end that the father knows more than he likes to let on. What is his attitude to the way he has changed, and his relationship within the marriage? Write either in a poem or prose, as if you were the father, about the way your life and marriage have developed.

Poetry Comparison 2: Seamus Heaney extracts

Before reading

How can you tell when you are reading a poem? Perhaps you expect it to look different on the page, or to have a special rhythm, or to rhyme. But what if it was set out like prose – like, say, the first page of an autobiography? Would you still be able to tell that it was a poem? Find out with these two texts.

Seamus Heaney is one of the most admired poets of the twentieth century. He also writes in prose (writing that is not poetry). Compare these two extracts describing some childhood memories. Both have been printed as if they were prose. But one is actually a poem. See if you can work out which.

What clues will you look for to see which text is poetry and which is prose?

Word bank
bole – tree-trunk
byre – barn
gnarled – knotted, twisted
inestimable – too great to calculate
jamb-wall – the wall next to the door
lithe – flexible
pith – soft tissue of the trunk
vibrant – moving as if alive

A Sofa in the Forties

All of us on the sofa in a line, kneeling behind each other, eldest down to youngest, elbows going like pistons, for this was a train and between the jamb-wall and the bedroom door our speed and distance were inestimable. First we shunted, then we whistled, then somebody collected the invisible for tickets and very gravely punched it as carriage after carriage under us moved faster, *chooka-chook*, the sofa legs went giddy and the unreachable ones far out on the kitchen floor began to wave.

Seamus Heaney

Mossbawn

All children want to crouch in their secret nests. I loved the fork of a beech tree at the head of our lane, the close thicket of a boxwood hedge in the front of the house, the soft, collapsing pile of hay in a back corner of the byre; but especially I spent time in the throat of an old willow tree at the end of the farmyard. It was a hollow tree, with gnarled, spreading roots, a soft, perishing bark and a pithy inside. Its mouth was like the fat and solid opening in a horse's collar, and, once you squeezed in through it, you were at the heart of a different life, looking out on the familiar yard as if it were suddenly behind a pane of strangeness. Above your head, the living tree flourished and breathed, you shouldered the slightly vibrant bole, and if you put your forehead to the rough pith you felt the whole lithe and whispering crown of willow moving in the sky above you.

Seamus Heaney

After reading

A

1 In a sentence, describe what happens in each text.

2 In 'A Sofa in the Forties', is Seamus Heaney recalling a happy or disturbing memory? How can you tell?

3 In 'Mossbawn', is he recalling a happy or disturbing memory? Again, how can you tell?

B

4 Choose one of the texts and write a brief paragraph about how Seamus Heaney makes his memories of childhood come alive. How does he make us feel as if we can actually see the scene that he is describing?

5 Which text do you prefer, and why?

Extended assignments

Both texts have been printed as if they were prose. One, in fact, is poetry. Which one? Have a go at writing it out as it would appear as a poem. Then write a brief paragraph explaining which clues suggested to you that it was poetry and which clues made the other text feel like prose.

Poetry Comparison 3: Thom Gunn and Louis MacNeice

Before reading

These two poems examine our earliest minutes of life and the promise, hopes and expectations that being born should hold for us. The writers' views, however, are not entirely positive ...

At the birth of a new baby, what would be your main wish for its future – health, wealth, happiness, peace, intelligence, ambition, security ...? Explain why.

Word bank
bureaucrats – officials of a large organization
dandle – comfort, play with
engendered – given birth
folly – madness
hector – bully
lure – tempt

Baby Song

From the private ease of Mother's womb
I fall into the lighted room.

Why don't they simply put me back
Where it is warm and wet and black?

But one thing follows on another
Things were different inside Mother.

Padded and jolly I would ride
The perfect comfort of her inside.

They tuck me in a rustling bed
– I lie there, raging, small, and red.

I may sleep soon, I may forget,
But I won't forget that I regret.

A rain of blood poured round her womb,
But all time roars outside this room.

Thom Gunn

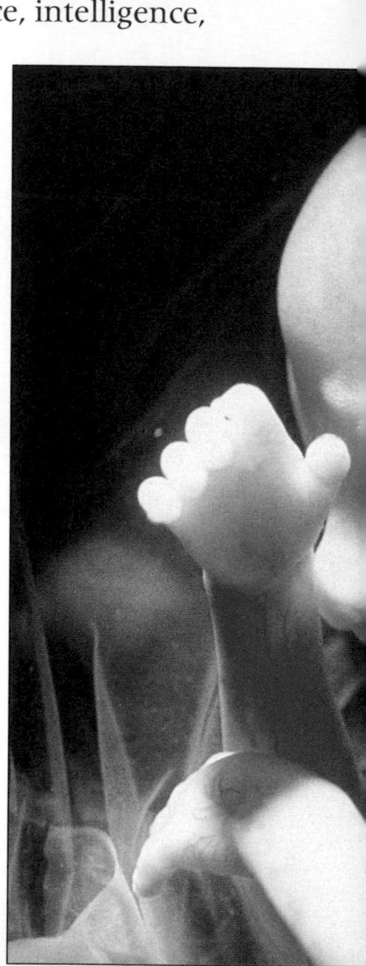

Prayer Before Birth

I am not yet born; O hear me.
Let not the bloodsucking bat or the rat or the stoat or the club-
footed ghoul come near me.

I am not yet born, console me.
I fear that the human race may with tall walls wall me,
with strong drugs dope me, with wise lies lure me,
on black racks rack me, in blood-baths roll me.

I am not yet born; provide me
With water to dandle me, grass to grow for me, trees to talk
to me, sky to sing to me, birds and a white light
in the back of my mind to guide me.

I am not yet born; forgive me
For the sins that in me the world shall commit, my words
when they speak me, my thoughts when they think me,
my treason engendered by traitors beyond me,
my life when they murder by means of my
hands, my death when they live me.

I am not yet born; rehearse me
In the parts I must play and the cues I must take when
old men lecture me, bureaucrats hector me, mountains
frown at me, lovers laugh at me, the white
waves call me to folly and the desert calls
me to doom and the beggar refuses
my gift and my children curse me.

I am not yet born; O hear me,
Let not the man who is beast or who thinks he is God
come near me.

Louis MacNeice

A: Baby Song

1 What do you suppose the 'lighted room' is in line 2?
2 Why does the baby wish to be back in its mother's womb?
3 Explain what you think the last two lines mean.
4 The poem is written in a series of rhyming couplets (pairings of lines that rhyme: 'womb ... room' and so on). Read them through again to yourself. How does this style contribute to the effect of the poem overall?

A: Prayer Before Birth

5 The baby keeps repeating the words 'O hear me'. Who do you think s/he might be addressing?

6 The poem reads as a list of desires and fears. What would you say is the main wish of the narrator – to be left alone, to be given good advice, to be protected from harmful influences, to be given support? Explain your choice.

B: Prayer Before Birth

7 How does the writer build a sense of rhythm as the poem develops?

8 How does the complex, repetitive style add to the message of the poem?

B: Comparison

9 In both poems, the young narrators express their hopes. What are the similarities and differences between these hopes?

10 Compare the language of the two poems. Look again at each poem and make notes on what you notice about:

- the structure
- vocabulary
- images
- rhythm
- rhyme.

Then use your notes to describe as precisely as you can what is similar and different in the language of each poem. Conclude by saying which poem you prefer.

1 Write your own 'Prayer Before Birth'. What would you wish for in the future of a soon-to-be-born baby? Write it as an essay or a speech.

2 Choose the poem you prefer and write about it, taking the reader through it a line at a time. What do you notice about the meaning, the writer's tone, the language he uses, the rhythm of the poem, the vocabulary, any changes in mood and developments of new ideas ... and so on.
Try to respond as precisely as you can to the writer's language. Conclude with your comments about the poem as a whole – what you particularly like or dislike about it.

NON-FICTION

Reading and responding to non-fiction texts

This section contains a range of non-fiction texts, including:

- a variety of genres – newspaper articles, advertisements, autobiography, travel writing, letters, leaflets, and speeches
- texts from this century and from the past
- texts from different cultures (for example, the USA, India, Africa, Britain)
- extracts and whole texts

There is a huge variety of non-fiction texts and we read them for all kinds of reasons. Some are intended to entertain us (for example, travel writing and autobiography). Others are chiefly aimed at informing us (leaflets, brochures, and newspaper articles). Some have a persuasive purpose – they want to change the way we think and feel (speeches and advertisements).

Of course, many non-fiction texts will have more than one purpose. A good newspaper story will do more than give us facts. It will also make us want to keep reading, using devices to tell its story in an interesting way.

This section gives you the chance to develop your confidence in reading non-fiction and, importantly, to compare the 'feel' of different genres of texts. With non-fiction, perhaps more than any other written form, it is important to keep asking yourself who the text is aimed at – who its audience is. This is an important element in deciding how successful it is.

Key skills

- Gaining confidence in reading non-fiction texts.
- Improving your understanding of the structure and style of a variety of texts.
- Comparing texts in the same genre.
- Thinking about audience, purpose, and tone.
- Developing your ability to describe your response as precisely as possible.

'I Killed the Loch Ness Monster'

Genre key: Newspaper article

It is difficult to sum up this category of writing. There are as many newspaper articles as there are newspaper readers. It depends which newspaper they are in, what the story is, whether it is serious or not, who the readers are ... and so on. But their main purpose, usually, will be to inform the reader.

Before reading

The newspaper article opposite is taken from an American newspaper called *The Weekly World News*. As you read, see whether you believe the story ...

What do you know about the legend of the Loch Ness monster?

Have you heard of any evidence that there might really be a monster down there under the water?

After reading

A

1 Who says that he has killed the Loch Ness Monster? Fill in this table of facts about him:

Name:	
Age:	
Job:	

2 Pick out a sentence which shows how this person feels about what he has done.

3 What facts are given about the monster? Make a list.

4 Why has the 'killer' now decided to own up?

B

5 Do you believe that this is a true story? What are the facts for and against? Look at the facts that are given, the comments of the people involved, and the use of photographs. Fill in this table to show your response:

Could be true	Probably false

Boat captain says he harpooned 62-foot creature by accident!

I KILLED THE LOCH NESS MONSTER

Dr Karl Cramer

by Sandra Lee
Weekly World News

GLASGOW, Scotland – In a shocking confession, the captain of a salvage boat has come forward to admit: 'I killed the Loch Ness Monster.'

'The fact that it was totally an accident does not ease my pain,' Ian Horwood said at a press conference. 'It has gotten to the point where I can't keep this a secret any longer.'

The death of the 62-foot, 1,000-year-old creature made headlines around the world in February when Dr Karl Cramer came forward with the shocking news – and a tragic photo of Nessie lying on a Loch Ness beach, slowly dying.

At the same time, Dr Cramer said the cause of death was unknown but indicated he believed 'an injury or illness' may have been to blame.

But now it turns out Dr Cramer was aware the monster died from being shot in the neck with a harpoon. The wound caused tremendous blood loss.

Horwood, 53, now admits that he inflicted the wound.

'I was on my salvage boat with three crew members and we were far out in the water looking for a boat that had gone down three weeks earlier,' he said. 'The sun was setting and we were getting ready to head for shore when the bottom of the boat was hit by something.

'Naturally I was startled and I grabbed my harpoon gun,' he said.

'Normally I don't have much use for the gun but in my business you always have to be prepared to protect yourself,' Horwood said. 'And I sometimes have problems with thieves when I'm out on my boat.'

Horwood said after the initial bump, nothing happened for a few minutes. But when the boat got near shore it started to rock violently.

'It was clear we had hit something – or something had hit us,' he said. 'I was out on the deck trying to figure out the situation when suddenly this giant creature rose up right in front of me.

'I admit it was frightening and I instinctively fired the harpoon at him. It all happened so fast I didn't have time to think.'

Horwood said he saw his harpoon hit the monster in the neck.

'After it fell down into the water, a crew member shined a powerful light on it and I realized then what I had done. I had shot the Loch Ness Monster.'

After returning to shore, Horwood debated with himself over what to do. But his worst nightmare came true two days later when Nessie washed up on a beach.

'I didn't know what to do,' he said. 'I had killed a national treasure.'

Horwood said he met with his crew members and they decided to keep their secret to themselves.

'We all had families to support and none of us wanted to go to jail,' he said. 'But as time has gone on, the guilt has become too much for me. I am ready to face my punishment.'

Ironically Horwood may not be punished at all. Because the Loch Ness Monster is a unique creature, prosecutors in Scotland say they are doubtful they can find a law that Horwood has broken.

But Dr Cramer said he is relieved the mystery is finally solved. 'We felt all along Nessie died a terrible death,' he said. 'We didn't want to say anything that would alarm the public until we were certain.

'Now we can finally close the chapter on this amazing creature.'

6 Now using your table of evidence, write a paragraph which explains your overall response to the article. If you think it is probably a true story, say why. If you think it's a hoax, say why. Try to support your opinion with evidence from the newspaper story.

Extended assignments

1 Imagine you are a scientist who wants to investigate whether the newspaper story is true. Write a letter to the captain asking him for more information about what happened. You might start it like this:

> Dear ...
>
> I have just read the report in the Weekly World News about the killing of the Loch Ness Monster. I am investigating what happened. Please would you answer the following questions ...

2 Why do you think some newspapers carry stories like this? Are they designed just to entertain us, rather than inform? Write a letter of complaint to the newspaper editor saying why you think there are more important issues in the world that could be covered.

Advice panel: responding to non-fiction

Remember to ask yourself:

- who was this text written for (what type of reader – age-
- group, special interests, etc.)?
- what is the purpose of the text – to give information, persuade, entertain ...?
- how is language used – short, snappy sentences and paragraphs, use of bullet-points? Is the vocabulary easy to understand or complex? Is the tone chatty or formal, serious or jokey?
- What do you notice about the layout of the text? How do the pictures and writing go together? What impression does the design give – childish, sophisticated, factual, colourful, lively, dull ...?

Playing Hopscotch 'Can Make Children Brainy'

Before reading

This article from a local newspaper is all about hopscotch. It says that playing hopscotch can make children better at school.

What do you know about the game hopscotch? If you had to tell someone what the point of the game was, what would you say?

Do you think this will be a serious story or some kind of joke?

Word bank
centenary – one hundredth anniversary
child psychologist – someone who studies children's behaviour
physiologist – someone who studies how people's bodies function

Playing hopscotch 'can make children brainy'

by Nicole Veash

Today's children are a sophisticated bunch, preferring the computer console to a game of hopscotch.

But the toys of the 21st century are causing problems for youngsters, say teachers from York's junior schools.

Dean Beecham, head of Bishopthorpe Junior School, said: 'Children seem to have less listening ability than they used to.

'We are worried this may be due to video games or watching too much television.'

Teachers believe that traditional games like hopscotch, skipping and catch could expand children's interests and stimulate their minds.

'Playground equipment tends not to be used, and the children just hang around and talk,' said Mr Beecham.

Dr Michael Bolton, a child psychologist from Keele University, said, 'If children spend a lot of time on their own in front of the TV or the computer, then any benefit they might have got from interacting with their peers will be lost.'

Clare Davison, a teacher at Fishergate Primary School, York, said, 'Last year in our centenary celebrations, the children looked at life in the Victorian age and learned about the games they played.

'Now they sometimes play hoops and hopscotch and their learning abilities seem to have improved.'

At Fishergate, the importance of play is also stressed in the classroom.

Ms Davison said: 'We have had assemblies on playing and we play games in lessons.

'Their co-operation skills are better and their academic ability has been stimulated because of this.'

Teachers at Bishopthorpe are so keen to bring active play back into their children's lives, they have launched a scheme to raise money for new equipment.

Gareth Stratton, a physiologist from the John Moore's University in Liverpool, said: 'If you keep children busy with physical exercise there is some evidence to suggest that their behaviour will be better and their minds more creative.'

He added: 'Computers can be good for learning if they are not just used for games, especially if children use CD Roms.'

How to play hopscotch

Start by chalking a series of squares on the ground, numbering them one to ten as shown on the left.

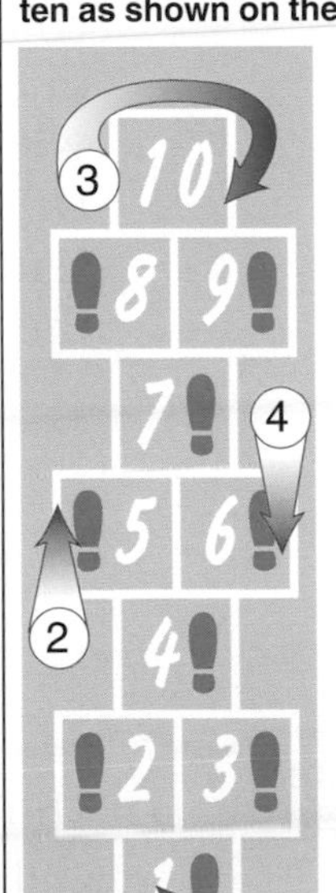

1. **Throw a stone into the first square.**
2. **Hop and skip from single to double squares respectively, without touching any of the chalk lines. Your starting square should be the one into which the stone was thrown.**
3. **On the tenth square, you must turn around without placing your other foot on the ground.**
4. **Hop and skip back to your starting square. Repeat the process for each of the other players.**
5. **Throw the stone into square number two.**
6. **Repeat this sequence for each of the ten squares and each player.**

Note: There are regional variations to this game.

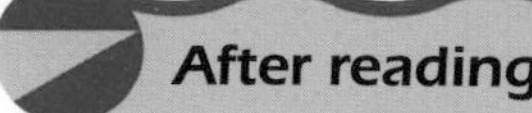

After reading

A

1 Based on the comments in the article, fill in this table:

Arguments in favour of playing more traditional games	Arguments against using computers	Arguments in favour of computers

2 Which experts say that hopscotch may make children learn more successfully?

3 Look at the end of the hopscotch rules. It says, 'There are regional variations to this game.' What do you think this might mean?

B

4 The writer has collected the opinions of teachers and behaviour experts. Is there anyone else's opinion which might have been useful?

5 The headline states that 'Playing hopscotch can make children brainy'. Is this what the article is actually saying, or could the headline be more accurate? If you are happy with the headline, write a sentence or two saying why. Otherwise, write a new headline and, beneath it, write a sentence or two saying why you think yours is better than the original.

Extended assignments

1 Think of one or two other traditional games you played in childhood – e.g. tag, hide and seek. Write a page of instructions for a new reference book, using illustrations if you want, to show people how the games work.

2 Do you agree with the article? If not, write a letter to the newspaper saying why not and giving your opinions about traditional games and computers. Begin your letter to the editor: 'Dear Sir/Madam, I have just read Nicole Veash's article about hopscotch and ...'

Crime-hit US City Clears its Streets of Children

Before reading

This article from the *Guardian* newspaper describes the way curfews are being used to clear American streets of crime. Anyone below a certain age is expected to be off the streets by a stated time.

Does this sound like a good idea to you? What arguments for and against it can you think of?

The Guardian Saturday June 1 1996

Daytime ban added to night curfew on under-18s in New Jersey

Crime-hit US city clears its streets of children

Jonathan Freedland in Washington

A New Jersey city plagued by crime has taken the dramatic step of reinforcing its night-time curfew on all children under 18 with a daytime ban as well – leaving them free for just 10 hours a day.

Faced with drug trafficking and gang violence by night and school truancy by day, the authorities in Camden, New Jersey will now bar all children between the ages of five and 18 from the streets from 8.30am until 3pm – adding to the ban already in force between 10pm and 6am. Parents of those caught will face a fine of £650 or up to 90 days in jail.

The drastic action was announced the day after President Clinton's call to combat youth violence with night-time curfews, which alarmed civil liberties groups and child rights advocates who fear it could lead to a virtual ban on all under-18s from America's streets.

The president's support for so-called 'teen curfews' – already in force in three quarters of America's largest 200 cities – has touched off a hotly contested debate, with critics charging that much-celebrated gains have been exaggerated and real costs ignored.

Cities from Washington DC to Denver have introduced laws banning children from staying out after dark, with most authorities imposing heavy fines for each violation.

A curfew scheme in New Orleans drew particular praise from President Clinton. Since 1994, the city has required all under-17s to be off the streets by 8pm on a winter school night, 9pm in summer. At the weekend, teenagers not indoors by 11pm are taken to a 'central curfew centre', where their parents must pick them up. The whole family must then undergo counselling. The night-time youth crime rate in New Orleans has fallen by 27 per cent.

'These are just like the old-fashioned rules most of us had when we were kids,' Mr Clinton told a conference of church leaders in Louisiana on Thursday. Recalling the words of his late mother, he said, 'When the lights come on, be home, Bill.'

With thousands of parents and families gathering in Washington today for a rally at the Lincoln Memorial called to protest against Republican cuts in services for children, the president's remarks have renewed an often bitter debate about American youth, who are disproportionally involved in crime both as victims and perpetrators.

Advocates brandish statistics showing considerable declines in rates of crime and violence where curfews are in force. As violent crime among teens rose 57 per cent between 1984 and 1994, even while the general US crime rate slowed, a pro-curfew consensus has evolved among US mayors.

'They keep our children out of harm's way,' said Mr Clinton, who is using the issue to highlight his tough-love approach to crime in this year's presidential election campaign. The president pointedly did not suggest a new national law, or even federal funds for curfews. Instead he merely encouraged cities to take up the idea.

'Curfews sound good,' said sociologist Ruth Sidel. 'It's a touchy-feely solution which makes people feel better, but it doesn't really solve the problems most kids face today.'

Ms Sidel fears curfews discriminate against poor kids, because they rarely have parents able to chauffeur them around and keep them off the streets. 'Upper middle class teenagers will always have mummy or daddy to drive them to band practice,' she said.

Jim Weill, of the Children's Defence Fund, the main organizers of today's march, said he was also concerned that curfews do not deal with the most troublesome children. 'The toughest kids are not in places where police are likely to pick them up, because they're simply too streetwise,' he said.

But the harshest criticism has come from the American Civil Liberties Union. 'What these laws do is penalize normal and otherwise lawful behaviour, for example standing on the street corner, and penalize the many for the misdeeds of the few,' said activist Norman Siegle.

'You're sending a really horrible message to a younger generation that the solution to a problem is repression,' he told the New York Times.

'These are just like the old-fashioned rules most of us had when we were kids'

Word bank

advocates – supporters
brandish – show off
Lincoln Memorial – landmark in Washington DC, capital city of the USA
New Jersey – American state near New York
perpetrators – offenders (those who commit the crimes)

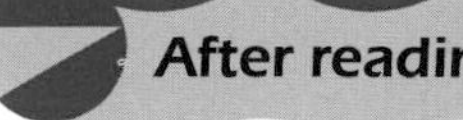

After reading

A

1 What problems are curfews aimed at solving?
2 How does the curfew idea work? Use these sentence starters to define their effect:
   - Curfews are designed to ...
   - Young people in curfew zones are expected to ...
   - If they don't obey the curfews ....
3 What is Bill Clinton doing to support the curfew idea?
4 What, according to the article, is he not doing?

B

5 Based upon your reading, fill in this table:

Arguments for the night curfews	Arguments against them

6 Several opinions are quoted in the article. Whose do you most agree with? Why?
7 Is the newspaper reporter neutral or biased? How can you tell?

Extended assignments

1 Write a letter to the newspaper giving the point of view of a young person affected by the curfew idea. Explain why you think it is unfair.
2 Imagine a discussion between a strong supporter of the curfew idea and a fierce opponent. Place them in a television or radio debate and script the conversation they have. Make each one give as many factual details as possible, drawn from the article.

Nicholas Fisk: Pig Ignorant

Genre key: Autobiography

Writing autobiographies helps us to put our life into some kind of order. We can look at the patterns of what has happened to us and remember the best and worst of times.

We probably read them because human beings are fascinated by other people's lives.

Before reading

Nicholas Fisk is the author of many books for young people. His most famous is probably *Grinny* – about a space alien who comes to earth disguised as a Great Aunt. This extract is from Nicholas Fisk's autobiography, *Pig Ignorant,* about his days growing up in London. It describes a typical mealtime.

Who do you live with at home? Think about how your relationship with her or him has changed as you have grown up. Then look at Nicholas Fisk's relationship with his mother ...

Pig Ignorant

Word bank
countenance – face, expression
intones – speaks in a single-tone voice
leadenly – heavily
mahogany – dark, heavy wood

He's late! His mother and his sister are already sitting at the round mahogany dining-room table. And they've started eating.

His mother, without looking up, asks, all on one note, 'What is the time?'

'Er... er...' he says, looking at his watch, which shows one twenty-six. 'Just after twenty past one.'

'Lunch in this house,' intones his mother, 'is at a quarter past one.'

She speaks in the voice of a judge passing sentence on a particularly disgusting criminal. Silently, Nick seats himself, eyes downcast, and picks up knife and fork. Noisily, he fumbles the fork and it clatters and rings on the table. His mother flinches at, but bravely bears, the noise. 'After lunch,' she announces, 'I am going to have a little lie-down. I have one of my headaches.'

Nick rams food down his throat. He glances across the table at his sister. She has a round, blonde, delightful face, but there is no delight in it at this moment: it wears the expression so often seen – the guarded, careful 'Really-I'm-perfectly-at-ease' look, the dull cheerfulness of a dutiful daughter. A saintly look. But then, she is a saint compared with her devil of a brother, who, in time with every chew, is silently reciting 'Bugger... bugger... bugger...'

He steals a glance at his mother, a handsome woman who once must have been a beauty. She has a large body, a sensitive countenance and particularly elegant, slender hands, marred only

by a slight orange-brown staining of two fingers. She gets through twenty or more Players full-strength cigarettes a day.

They cost 11½d. The ½d change buys a D-section finger of Cadbury's milk chocolate. Delicious. Even at his advanced age – sixteen and a half, remember – Nick still relishes the halfpennyworth, his reward for cycling to the shop for another packet of twenty.

The meal ends with tinned tangerines and 'coffee cream' – single cream. Tinned tangerines are still a delicacy to him. He almost cheers up. But then the awful weight of his mother's voice descends on him again: 'I'll leave you two to do the washing-up,' it leadenly pronounces. It might just as well have added, 'And you will hang by the neck until you are dead.'

Exit mother. Son and daughter enter the scullery, crockery loaded on tray. Now Nick is scowling and gnashing his teeth, furious with himself for being furious. 'Why *must* she carry on like that?' he demands. 'All that doom and gloom just because I'm a few minutes late!'

'You must remember,' his sister says piously, 'that she's had a lot to put up with since Father died.'

There's no answer to that: it is obviously true. And yet...

'You can wash if you like,' said his sister. 'I don't mind drying and putting away.'

She really is a saint.

Meanwhile, here's good old Peter at the door. 'Want to come up west with me? The Cameo's showing six cartoons – all Disney!'

'OK, hang on, I'll get my cycle clips.'

Has Nick enough money for an hour of cartoons? He'll need a shilling (five pence today). Ah, terrific, here's a florin – a ten-pence piece. They're off and away, riding through the slow-moving, easy traffic, through Hammersmith, Earls Court, Kensington, to Piccadilly.

They lean their bikes against the railings around the little cinema. They don't bother to lock them. They buy a tuppenny Mars bar each; and laugh through an hour of Mickey Mouse, Donald Duck and Goofy.

There is a newsreel, too, all about Herr Hitler and his tanks and torchlit, goose-stepping processions (but the tanks are just cardboard, everyone says so).

Nicholas Fisk

A

1 Find a sentence in the extract which shows that Nick is hurrying his food.

2 What do we learn about the different members of Nick's family? Make a list of points under each of these headings. Mention what the people look like, how they talk, how they get on with each other, how they behave ... anything which you learn from the text.

Mother	Sister	Nick

3 How does Nick's sister explain the way their mother behaves?

4 Pick out a sentence which you think best sums up Nick's attitude to his mother.

B

5 What impression do you get of the lifestyle of the family? What do they eat? What kind of house do they live in? Are they wealthy or poor? How can you tell? Write a brief paragraph about what you notice.

6 What clues are there about *when* the extract takes place? Find as many specific examples as you can which show the period it is set in.

7 Although this is an autobiography, Nicholas Fisk uses the third-person form ('he') rather than the first-person ('I').
- What effect does this have?
- How do we react differently to what he shows us?
- What advantages and disadvantages might it have as a way of telling your life-story?

The extract is also written in the present tense ('Nick rams food down his throat ...') although the events it describes are set in the past. What effect does this style have?
Write a paragraph exploring Nicholas Fisk's style in response to these questions.

1 How would the scene at the dinner-table be told differently by Nick's mother or his sister? Choose one of these two people, and describe the same event from their point of view. In particular, describe how Nick eats his food, how he behaves, and what the atmosphere is like. Try to show what you are feeling inside during the meal.

2 If you were writing your own autobiography, you would probably write saying 'I ...' and 'me'. But Nicholas Fisk uses 'he' instead. Have a go at writing a moment from your own life using this style. Choose a moment when you got in trouble or were late or got a telling-off. Try to use details of people and places to make the story come to life – make sure the reader can see what you remember.

Blake Morrison: And When Did You Last See Your Father?

Before reading

Most of us remember times when a parent behaved in a way that embarrassed us. Here Blake Morrison thinks back to his father and the way he couldn't stand to be kept waiting in queues ...

Think of a time when you were embarrassed by a parent's behaviour. What did you do – hide your feelings or make it clear how you felt?

And When Did You Last See Your Father?

Word bank

convertible – car with a soft-top roof to be drawn back in good weather
incenses – makes him furious
magnanimous – generous
non-sequitur – two ideas which have no obvious connection
pall – shroud or cloak
plebs – ordinary people (short for *plebeians*)
speculation – thought
stationary – standing still
tantalizingly – as if teasing him
undemocratic – unfair

A hot September Saturday in 1959, and we are stationary in Cheshire. Ahead of us, a queue of cars stretches out of sight around the corner. We haven't moved for ten minutes. Everyone has turned his engine off, and now my father does so too. In the sudden silence we can hear the distant whinge of what must be the first race of the afternoon, a ten-lap event for saloon cars. It is quarter past one. In an hour the drivers will be warming up for the main event, the God Cup – Graham Hill, Jack Brabham, Roy Salvadori, Stirling Moss and Joakim Bonnier. My father has always loved fast cars, and motor-racing has a strong British following just now, which is why we are stuck here in this country lane with hundreds of other cars.

My father does not like waiting in queues. He is used to patients waiting in queues to see him, but he is not used to waiting in queues himself. A queue, to him, means a man being denied the right to be where he wants to be at a time of his own choosing, which is at the front, now. Ten minutes have passed. What is happening up ahead? What fathead has caused this snarl-up? Why are no cars coming the other way? Has there been an accident? Why are there no police to sort it out? Every two minutes or so my father gets out of the car, crosses to the opposite verge and tries to see if there is movement up ahead. There isn't. He gets back in and steams some more. The roof of our Alvis is down, the sun beating on to the leather upholstery, the chrome, the picnic basket. The hood is folded and pleated into the mysterious crevice between the boot and the narrow back seat where my sister and I are crunched together as usual. The roof is nearly always down, whatever the weather: my father loves fresh air, and every car he has owned has been a convertible, so that he can have fresh air. But the air today is not fresh. There is a pall of high-rev exhaust, dust, petrol, boiling-over engines.

In the cars ahead and behind, people are laughing, eating sandwiches, drinking from beer bottles, enjoying the weather, settling into the familiar indignity of waiting-to-get-to-the-front.

But my father is not like them. There are only two things on his mind: the invisible head of the queue and, not unrelated, the other half of the country lane, tantalizingly empty.

'Just relax, Arthur,' my mother says. 'You're in and out of the car like a blue-tailed fly.'

But being told to relax only incenses him. 'What can it be?' he demands. 'Maybe there's been an accident. Maybe they're waiting for an ambulance.' We all know where this last speculation is leading, even before he says it. 'Maybe they need a doctor.'

'No, Arthur,' says my mother, as he opens the door again and stands on the wheel-arch to crane ahead.

'It must be an accident,' he announces. 'I think I should drive up and see.'

'No, Arthur. It's just the numbers waiting to get in. And surely there must be doctors on the circuit.'

It is one-thirty and silent now. The saloon race has finished. It is still over an hour until the Gold Cup itself, but there's another race first, and the cars in the paddock to see, and besides...

'Well, I'm not going to bloody well wait here any longer,' he says. 'We'll never get in. We might as well turn round and give up.' He sits there for another twenty seconds, then leans forward, opens the glove compartment and pulls out a stethoscope, which he hooks over the mirror on the windscreen. It hangs there like a skeleton, the membrane at the top, the metal and rubber leads dangling bow-legged, the two ivory earpieces clopping bonily against each other. He starts the engine, releases the handbrake, reverses two feet, then pulls out into the opposite side of the road.

'No,' says my mother again, half-heartedly. It could be that he is about to do a three-point turn and go back. No it couldn't...

My father does not drive particularly quickly past the marooned cars ahead. No more than twenty miles an hour. Even so, it *feels* fast, and arrogant, and all the occupants turn and stare as they see us coming. Some appear to be angry. Some are shouting. 'Point to the stethoscope, pet,' he tells my mother, but she has slid down sideways in her passenger seat, out of sight, her bottom resting on the floor, from where she berates him.

'God Almighty, Arthur, why do you have to do this? Why can't you wait like everyone else? What if we meet something coming the other way?' Now my sister and I do the same, hide ourselves below the seat. Our father is on his own. He is not with us, this bullying, shaming undemocratic cheat. Or rather, we are not with him.

My face pressed to the sweet-smelling upholstery, I imagine

what is happening ahead. I can't tell how far we have gone, how many blind corners we have taken. If we meet something, on this narrow country lane, we will have to reverse past all the cars we have just overtaken. That's if we can stop in time. I wait for the squeal of brakes, the clash of metal.

After an eternity of – what? – two minutes, my mother sticks her head up and says, 'Now you've had it,' and my father replies, 'No, there's another gate beyond,' and my sister and I raise ourselves to look. We are up level with the cars at the head of the queue, which are waiting to turn left into the brown ticket holders' entrance, the plebs' entrance. A steward steps out of the gateway towards us, but my father, pretending not to see him, doesn't stop. He drives ahead, on to a clear piece of road where, two hundred yards away, half a dozen cars from the opposite direction are waiting to turn into another gateway. Unlike those we have left behind, these cars appear to be moving. Magnanimous, my father waits until the last of them has turned in, then drives through the stone gateposts and over the bumpy grass to where an armbanded steward in a tweed jacket is waiting by the roped entrance.

'Good afternoon, sir. Red ticket holder?' The question does not come as a shock: we have all seen the signs, numerous and clamorous, saying RED TICKET HOLDERS' ENTRANCE. But my father is undeterred.

'These, you mean,' he says, and hands over his brown tickets.

'No, sir. I'm afraid these are brown tickets.'

'But there must be some mistake. I applied for red tickets. To be honest, I didn't even look.'

'I'm sorry, sir, but these are brown tickets, and brown's the next entrance, two hundred yards along. If you just swing round here, and ...'

'I'm happy to pay the difference.'

'No, you see the rules say...'

'I know where the brown entrance is, I've just spent the last hour queuing for it by mistake. I drove up here because I thought I was red. I can't go back there now. The queue stretches for miles. And these children, you know, who'd been looking forward...'

By now half a dozen cars have gathered behind us. One of them parps. The steward is wavering.

'You say you applied for red.'

'Not only applied for, paid for. I'm a doctor, you see' – he points at the stethoscope – 'and I like being near the grand-stand.'

This double non-sequitur seems to clinch it.

'All right, sir, but next time please check the tickets. Ahead and to your right.'

Blake Morrison

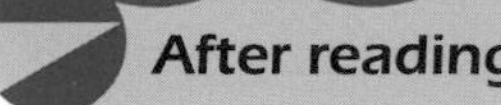

After reading

A

1 Who is in the car?
2 Why are they heading to a motor-racing event?
3 Use a table like the one below to list the information we learn about Blake Morrison's father:

Name	
Occupation	
Character	

4 Pick out a quotation which shows Blake Morrison's mother's reaction to what happens.

B

5 Why at the end of the extract do you think the steward lets the car through?
6 What advice would you give to the father about how he should have behaved in the queue?
7 Blake Morrison shows us how his mother reacts to his father's behaviour. But we see little of his own response. Look closely through the text for any clues about his feelings at what he sees. See if you can find clues about the feelings of Blake Morrison as a boy, and those he has now as an adult. Write a brief paragraph describing what you find.

Extended assignments

1 How do you think the family feel about what happens? Imagine the scene in the car after the day has finished. Write a description of part of the journey home, with the conversation between the mother and father and the reaction of Blake Morrison in the back. Try to capture the atmosphere of what it would have been like.
2 Imagine you are the steward who finally let the car through. Write about why you did this. Describe what you were doing before the Morrisons' car pulled up; your first impressions when you spoke to the father; how you tried to persuade him to turn back; how the other people in the car were reacting; why you finally decided to give in; whether you think it was the right thing to do.

Frances Ann Kemble: The Opening of the Liverpool to Manchester Railway

Before reading

Nowadays we take technology for granted, but people haven't always viewed it like this. This extract from the autobiography of Frances Ann Kemble recalls a dramatic moment from her life. Filled with excitement, in 1830 she joins the eight hundred people who travel on the first steam train on the new Liverpool to Manchester railway line. Delight turns to horror, when visiting politician William Huskisson is killed – one of the world's first railway disasters.

How do you imagine the crowds felt that day, as they waited to catch their first glimpse of the new invention, the steam engine? What must the mood have been like?

The Opening of the Liverpool to Manchester Railway

Word bank
annihilation – destruction
artisans – craftsmen
ascertain – find out
bewildered – confused
borne – carried
concourse – crowd
velocity – speed

The most intense curiosity and excitement prevailed, and, though the weather was uncertain, enormous masses of densely packed people lined the road, shouting and waving hats and handkerchiefs as we flew by them. What with the sight and sound of these cheering multitudes and the tremendous velocity with which we were borne past them, my spirits rose to the true champagne height, and I never enjoyed anything so much as the first hour of our progress. I had been unluckily separated from my mother in the first distribution of places, but by an exchange of seats which she was enabled to make she rejoined me when I was at the height of my ecstasy, which was considerably damped by finding that she was frightened to death, and intent upon nothing but devising means of escaping from a situation which appeared to her to threaten with instant annihilation herself and all her travelling companions. While I was chewing the cud of this disappointment, which was rather bitter, as I had expected her to be as delighted as myself with our excursion, a man flew by us, calling out through a speaking-trumpet to stop the engine, for that somebody in the directors' carriage had sustained an injury. We were all stopped accordingly, and presently a hundred voices were heard exclaiming that Mr Huskisson was killed; the confusion that ensued is indescribable; the calling out from carriage to carriage to ascertain the truth, the contrary reports which were sent back to us, the hundred questions eagerly uttered at once, and the repeated and urgent demands for surgical assistance, created a sudden turmoil that was quite sickening. At last we distinctly ascertained that the unfortunate man's thigh was broken. From Lady Wilton, who was in the Duke's carriage, and within three yards of the spot where the accident happened, I had the following details, the horror of witnessing which we were spared through our situation behind the great carriage. The engine had stopped to take in a supply of water, and several of the gentlemen in the directors' carriage had jumped out to look about them. Lord Wilton, Count Batthyany, Count Matuscenitz, and Mr Huskisson among the rest were standing talking in the middle of the road, when an engine on the other line, which was parading up and down merely to show its speed, was seen coming down upon them like lightning. The most active of those in peril sprang back into their seats; Lord Wilton saved his life only by rushing behind the Duke's carriage, and Count Matuscenitz had but just leaped into it, with the engine all but touching his heels as he did so; while poor Mr Huskisson, less active from the effects of age and ill-health, bewildered, too, by the frantic cries of 'Stop the engine! Clear the track!' that resounded on all sides, completely lost his head, looked helplessly to the right and left, and was instantaneously prostrated by the fatal machine, which dashed down like a thunderbolt upon, and passed over his leg, smashing and mangling it in the most horrible way. (Lady Wilton said she distinctly heard the crushing of the bone.) So terrible was the effect of the appalling accident that, except that ghastly 'crushing' and poor Mrs Huskisson's piercing shriek, not a sound was heard or a word uttered among the immediate spectators of the catastrophe. Lord Wilton was the first to raise the poor sufferer, and calling to aid his surgical skill, which is considerable, he tied up the severed artery and, for a time at least, prevented death by loss of blood. Mr Huskisson was then placed in a carriage with his wife and Lord Wilton, and the engine, having been detached from the directors' carriage, conveyed them to Manchester. So great was the shock produced upon the whole party by this event, that the Duke of Wellington declared his intention not to proceed, but to return immediately to Liverpool. However, upon its being represented to him that the whole population of Manchester had turned out to witness the procession, and that a disappointment might give rise to riots and disturbances, he consented to go on, and gloomily enough the rest of the journey was accomplished...

After this disastrous event the day became overcast, and as we neared Manchester the sky grew cloudy and dark, and it began to rain. The vast concourse of people who had assembled to witness the triumphant arrival of the successful travellers was of the lowest order of mechanics and artisans, among whom great distress and a dangerous spirit of discontent with the government at that time prevailed. Groans and hisses greeted the carriage, full of influential personages, in which the Duke of Wellington sat. High above the grim and grimy crowd of scowling faces a loom had been erected, at which sat a tattered, starved-looking weaver, evidently set there as a representative man, to protest against the triumph of machinery and the gain and glory which the wealthy Liverpool and Manchester men were likely to derive from it. The contrast between our departure from Liverpool and our arrival at Manchester was one of the most striking things I ever witnessed.

Frances Ann Kemble

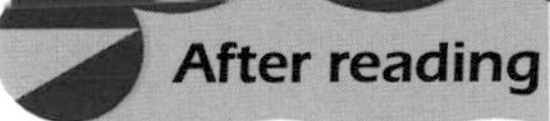

After reading

A

1 Choose a phrase or sentence from the extract which shows the early excitement of the crowd.
2 Choose a quotation from nearer the end of the text which shows how the people's mood has changed.
3 How does the writer's mother react to the day's adventure?
4 How do people react when the news first breaks that there has been an accident?

5 How does the writer feel about people's reactions?
6 How does the writer find out the truth of what happened?
7 Try to say, in one or two sentences only, what did happen to Mr Huskisson.
8 What do we learn about Mr Huskisson from the description of the accident?
9 The Duke of Wellington wants to cancel the rest of the journey. Why doesn't he do this?
10 What is the message of the 'starved-looking weaver' near the end of the extract?

B

11 What do we learn from the extract about Frances Ann Kemble?
12 The text was written in 1878. What clues can you find in the text as to its age?

1 Imagine the local newspaper's coverage of the disaster. Write the headline and 200-word story describing the day's events. Quote some of the eyewitnesses mentioned in Frances Ann Kemble's account.
2 Some people thought that the disaster supported their worries about so-called progress. Interview the weaver, at the end of the extract. Although he didn't see the accident, describe his thoughts about what he heard, how he reacted, and how he feels about technological progress.

Autobiography Comparison: Julia Strachey and Mulk Raj Anand

Before reading

These two accounts recall encounters with that most deadly of snakes – the cobra. Julia Strachey is living in India when, on a walk with her parents, the cobra appears. Mulk Raj Anand is imagining that he is the Indian hero of childhood stories, Raja Rasalu, when terror strikes ...

Do you share a horror of snakes? What is it that makes them so terrifying to many people? What do you know, in particular, about cobras?

Julia

Word bank
abnormal – unnatural
contortions – twisting movements
grotesque deformity – horribly ugly shape
intuitively – by instinct
jinns – spirits which can take human or animal form

I shall never forget the afternoon when I got my first sight of a cobra.

I was walking with my parents along a path that ran beside railings to the railway station. An old man holding a flute was squatting beside the path. On the ground beside him stood a tall rush-plaited basket with no lid to it. Only a narrow hole at the top. As we neared him the old man raised the flute to his lips and started to play a slow, rhythmical tune upon it. My parents, who recognized that a snake-charming performance was about to begin, came to a halt in front of the old fellow, thinking no doubt that the coming entertainment would delight me.

'Oh look, Ju! Look, look... you must see this!'

I looked and saw the neat little head of a serpent rise up with slow elegance from out the aperture at the top of the basket. As it rose ever higher and higher, the serpent started swaying his glittering black length from side to side in time to the flute music.

Had this been all of the performance I should have been well satisfied. But no! This kind of snake (which I had not come across before, and whose name of course was Cobra) had a peculiar – an exceptional – talent. I soon noticed that while the creature was so gracefully swaying from side to side to the rhythm of the flute, something weird and uncanny was happening at the same time. The narrow neat head began puffing itself out sideways – more and more and more. And still the head continued to swell! It was like a nightmare. It swelled. And swelled. And swelled. Changing its shape, changing its size, swelling larger and larger, ballooning itself up into the most infernal puffery – it became a black and glittering dinner plate, a grotesque deformity. Meanwhile a baleful hook-and-eye design began to manifest itself, slashed out big and bold across the snake's weirdly transformed head (if head it could still be called, for it had now reached unrecognizable proportions).

I had never seen anything like this happen before. And now the monstrous shape began hollowing and caving itself in, in a most uncanny way. Then I noticed with a start how its own former little modest snake face with the small beady eyes was now to be seen perched high up on the very top of this new giant face!

I had never before seen a spectacle so wicked and ferocious, so full of evil intent. I recognized Black Magic. A Demon casting straight at us a destructive spell. My heart twisted over and plummeted down into my boots, for I grasped intuitively that this crazed thing was actively menacing me, that all its abnormal contortions were aimed at destroying me!

'There's nothing to be afraid of! It's only dancing!' my mother and father tried to reassure me, looking down and seeing me between them in floods of tears.

Dancing it may have been! But this was plainly a ritual Dance of Death! And what can you do against that?

Julia Strachey

An Encounter

Through the deeps of stillness about me, disturbed only by a soft breeze in the hot sunny afternoon, I could hear the sound of water. I looked round and on the slopes of the dell at my feet I saw a crystal-clear pool issuing from some natural spring. I descended towards it through a little valley full of lush, tall grass, poppies, mushrooms and wild anemones. My heart pulled back with a sudden fear as I approached the water. But, recalling that Rasalu was very bold and not at all afraid of the wilds and forests, I took a palmful of water and drank to quench my thirst.

Then, still bound in the spell of my fancies, I capered here and there, exploring for the nest of a bird which I could hear cooing with a deep, resonant voice. But I could not locate it and sat down to rest under the scanty shade of a berry tree. The shrill cries of vultures haunted the landscape and filled it with the dread of a terrible desolation, especially as I had heard that vultures fed on corpses and lived in lonely places, haunted by jinns.

I got up and ran.

Hardly had I gone three steps when I heard a sudden, sinister whistle and saw, on one side, a long cobra creep out of a bush with its terrible, glistening black body and push its hood up with a flicker of its split tongues, as if it were full of a merciless anger and hate.

I stood transfixed for a moment and could not even shriek.

But the snake dipped its head and went its way into the bush grass where the frogs croaked.

I ran, shaking, terror-stricken and dumb.

Mulk Raj Anand

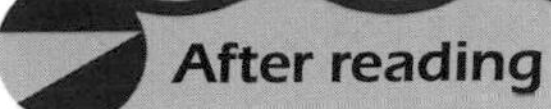

After reading

A

1 Look again at Julia Strachey's description of a cobra. Draw a quick sketch of what she describes and label its key features.

2 Now look at Mulk Raj Anand's much briefer description of a cobra. In a sentence say whether his account adds any new information about the cobra, or whether it simply confirms what Julia Strachey says.

3 Which description makes the cobra seem more terrifying? Why?

4 How do the two writers react to the sight of the snake? Who is more terrified?

B

5 Compare the way the two writers describe their feelings of fear.

6 What similarities and differences do you notice in the setting of each extract (where the encounters take place)?

7 Which text do you find more interesting, and why?

Extended assignments

1 The encounter with the cobra made a powerful impact on Julia Strachey's memory. Interview her about this experience from her childhood – what she recalls of the sight of the snake, her feelings then, and how she feels about cobras nowadays. Write it as a script.

2 Write about a time when you have been terrified by a creature – whether a spider, rat, or a herd of cows in a field you had to cross. Like the writers in these extracts, try to describe not only what you saw, but also what you felt like. Give as much detail as you can.

Kate Marsden: On Sledge and Horseback to Outcast Siberian Lepers

Genre key: Travel writing

Travel writing can have the feel of autobiography – 'This is what I did when I was in ...'. Sometimes it describes the journey itself. Sometimes it tells us about the writer's experience in other cultures. So in reading travel writing we have two interests: the writer and what the writer sees.

Before reading

Kate Marsden was a missionary. Here she travels into Siberia in search of a herb which is supposed to cure leprosy. Leprosy is a vicious disease which attacks a person's limbs, making them wither away. Kate Marsden never found the herb and never truly recovered from her journey of 1891. This account was written in 1921 and describes her distressing encounters with groups of leprosy victims.

What do you already know about the disease leprosy? Do you think it would be possible to write about a terrible disease without being depressing?

On Sledge and Horseback to Outcast Siberian Lepers

Word bank

callous – hard-hearted
cavalcade – procession
contagion – passing on the disease
contrive – manage
incessant – unceasing
lest – in case
myriads – great numbers, lots
putrid – rotten
Yakuts – a race of people from Siberia
yourta – circular skin- or felt-covered tent

We pushed our way through the usual dense forest, along the track which had been cleared for me by the kind natives, as I have already mentioned, and which otherwise would have been impassable. Halting at the leper settlement of Hatignach, a scene met my eyes too horrible to describe fully. Twelve men, women, and children, scantily and filthily clothed, were huddled together in two small yourtas, covered with vermin. The stench was dreadful; one man was dying, two men had lost their toes and half of their feet; they had tied boards from their knees to the ground, so that by this help they could contrive to drag themselves along. One man had no fingers; and the poor stumps, raised to make the sign of the cross, were enough to bring tears to the eyes of the most callous. On my approaching them they all crouched on the ground, as if almost terror-struck at the very idea of anyone coming near to help them. I gave them all the help possible, and then, with a smile on their faces, they looked and pointed heavenwards, trying to make me understand that they were praying for blessings on those who had considered their wants. In some cases the fur of the tattered clothes had stuck to the sores, thus causing intense irritation.

During the eight or nine months of winter, these people huddled together with the cattle as closely as possible in their dreadful hovels, in order to keep warm. They, too, had been attacked by typhus fever and smallpox. I said farewell, and, mounting my horse, heard angry words behind me. Turning round I found that some of the lepers wanted to come near to speak to me, and the Yakuts were driving them away in horror, fearful lest they might catch the disease. Of course, I quickly went to them. They pleaded hard that hospitals might be built speedily, and that they might be supplied with bread, because the food brought to them was generally putrid.

Then we set off for the next settlement, which was a hundred and fifty miles farther on. We travelled all night – in fact, the greater part of this journey had to be done by night on account of the intense heat during the day, and the incessant attacks of large horse-flies, as well as the myriads of other insects. We halted at Sredni Viluisk, which, although marked as a town on the map, is only a collection of a few dirty yourtas and one Government office. A man suspected of being a leper was brought to me, and, after examination by the doctor, the suspicion was soon confirmed. It was arranged that he should have a new yourta, and live in a leper settlement about fifty miles away.

'How is he to get there?' I asked; for I saw how deformed he was, and that parts of his feet and hands were gone.

'He is to walk,' was the reply.

This walking meant that the poor fellow would have to crawl or drag himself along fifty miles of forest. At last, it was suggested that he should be tied to the back of a bull, and the bull be led by a boy (the man's brother) with a long cord. After a deal of persuasion I got the people to provide a sledge, with plenty of straw, and a bull to draw it, as there were no horses to spare. This is only a typical example of how some of the lepers, almost unable to walk at all, are left to get as best they can into the far-off forest. If a woman becomes a leper, she, too, is sometimes placed or tied on a bare-backed bull, which is led by a man with a long rope. If the animal sinks into the marshes or bogs, it must struggle out without help, and if the woman falls off, the man would rather die than go and touch her in giving assistance. Such sufferings as these, I try to refer to calmly; but it is hard to do so. The reader can imagine, without my help, all that such outcasts are compelled to endure. What a difference the bare-backed bullock presents to the merciful contrivances for removing the wounded from the battle-field and the victims of accidents in our streets!

Another dreadful instance of what they had to endure was related to me. A leper woman was placed in a yourta with another leper, a man, who, soon after her arrival, became insane. For four

years this poor woman had to live with a madman in the depths of the forest, away from every human being, never sure from one hour to another of her life. Just picture the constant dread she must have lived in – at night, hardly daring to close her eyes to sleep; during the day, ever on the watch for each movement the man made, knowing well that, should he attack her, there was no hand to protect her, no ear to attend to her cries of help – for miles and miles around nothing but the dense forest to echo back her voice. As, bit by bit, this information was translated to me, a tremor went through my whole being; whilst, deep in my heart, I thanked God for sending me here to these helpless, forsaken ones.

Our midnight march from Sredni Viluisk was beset with dangers. We heard that bears were in the neighbourhood, and the horses kept on starting, and then darting to one side and the other. The trees loomed above us against the sky, the rotten roots and holes were under our feet, and on every hand was a dead silence.

After a long ride we came to nine more lepers, whose condition was worse than any I had seen. Two women, one man of about forty, and two children were naked, having no clothes whatsoever; and, with the exception of a few rags, they are in the same state in the winter. During the months of biting frost, all the covering they had was hay and rags. As I sat there amongst them, the flies were tormenting their festering wounds, and some of the outcasts writhed in agony. I do not wonder at being told that it was impossible to reach the lepers, for this was another settlement hidden away in the forest, with no path or communication of any kind to other places. There were traces of a bear here, and I began to wonder why some of these lepers did not, in their desperation, throw themselves in the way of the bears, and so end their miseries.

As we again mounted our horses, the Yakuts, who had kept far off from the lepers for fear of contagion, hurried on the animals in order to get away from the place as quickly as possible. As we rode forward in the darkness, the faces of those poor creatures haunted me; whilst now and then an owl hooted, or a savage rat darted at my horse, making him plunge and struggle. We kept struggling into holes and over roots of trees, and it was as much as a tired, aching woman could do to keep her seat. Then two of the horses took fright; and, all the horses being tied in a single file by tail and bridle, the whole cavalcade rushed along full tilt into the darkness, and we were simply at God's mercy. When we went steadily again, and silence reigned around, how my full heart was lifted up to God! When going at full speed, the horses would suddenly stop; then a wild goose would screech and flutter his wings, and on we would tear again.

Kate Marsden

After reading

A

1 Choose one detail from the first paragraph which shows Kate Marsden's caring attitude to the leprosy victims.

2 Choose three details – for example, animals the author mentions, or words the author uses – which show that the events take place in Russia.

3 Write down three facts about the disease leprosy which you learn from the extract.

4 'Turning round I found some of the lepers wanted to come near to speak to me, and the Yakuts were driving them away in horror, fearful lest they might catch the disease.' Think of three words or phrases to describe what this quotation shows about Kate Marsden.

B

5 Which part of the text do you find most disturbing or upsetting? Try to explain why.

6 Do you admire Kate Marsden, or are there parts of her character which are less likeable? Write about your response to her, giving examples.

Extended assignments

1 Imagine Kate Marsden arriving home from her expedition to Siberia. Create an interview with her exploring her feelings about what she has seen and how she feels the journey has changed her.

2 Write in detail about your response to Kate Marsden's account. What have you learnt from it? What impression do you gain of her? What do you notice about her written style? Which parts do you find most/least effective?

Letters Comparison: Fergal Keane

Genre key: Letters Letters can be fairly dull to the outsider – writing to ask for information, writing to complain, writing with holiday news. These things may be interesting to us if we are the writer, or if the letter is addressed to us. Some letters, though, have wider interest and, like autobiographies and travel writing, they can inform, entertain, terrify and shock us. Most letters belong in their time-period. The best ones live on and speak to future generations.

Before reading

Fergal Keane is a journalist with the BBC. The birth of his new son makes him think back to his troubled relationship with his father. He writes a letter to both – to his dead father and new-born son.

What kinds of emotions do you expect to find in the letters? How do you think the two letters will differ?

Dear Father

Dublin, New Year's Day 1972

Behind the bedroom door you are sleeping. I can hear your snores rattling down the stairs to our ruined sitting room. Here among the broken chairs, the overturned Christmas tree, we are preparing to leave you. We are breaking away from you, Da.

Last night you crashed through the silence, dead drunk and spinning in your own wild orbit into another year of dreams. This would be the year of the big break – of Hollywood, you said. Oh my actor father, time was, time was, we swallowed those lines – but no longer.

Before leaving I look into the bedroom to where your hand droops out from under the covers, below it the small empty Powers' bottle, and I say goodbye.

And at seven o'clock on New Year's day we push the old Ford Anglia down the driveway – my mother, brother and I. We push because the engine might wake you, and none of us can face a farewell scene. I don't know what the neighbours think, if anything, when they see a woman and two small boys stealing away in the grey morning, but I don't care, we're heading south with everything we own.

The day I turned 12, which was four days later, you called to say happy birthday. You were, as I remember, half-way sober, but you didn't say much else, except to ask for my mother, who would not come to the phone.

In the background I could hear glasses clinking, voices raised, and you said: 'Tell her I love her,' and then the change ran out, and I began to understand what made love the saddest word in any language.

Christmas that year, and you had access to the children. We met in Cork Station. I remember your new suit, your embarrassed embrace, the money you pressed into our hands, and the smell of whisky. We found a taxi and the driver stared at us, throwing his eyes to heaven and shaking his head.

What I see now are many such faces; the waitress at the Old Bridge Café where drinks were spilled; the couple who asked for an autograph and watched your shaking hand struggle to write, before they beat a mortified retreat.

And on through pubs and bookie shops to one last café where Elvis was crooning 'Love Me Tender, Love Me Sweet' on an ancient radio, by now, nobody able to speak.

There was a taxi ride home, we children in the back, you in the front, and what lives with me still, always, is the moment of leave taking, Christmas 1972. Because as the car drove away from our lives I saw through the steamed-up windows that your eyes had become waterfalls.

I was too young to understand what you knew – we were lost to you, broken away. Down the years we struggled to find one another, but I was growing up and away, and you were drifting closer to darkness. And at the end I gave up writing, gave up calling. I gave up.

Until one night my cousin called to say you were gone. It was a few days after Christmas, and your heart simply gave up in a small room in the town in north Kerry where you were born. I remember that you sent me the collected stories of Raymond Carver for Christmas. I had sent you nothing, not even a card. Now I would send you a thousand but I have no address.

Fergal

My Dear Son

Hong Kong

It is six o'clock in the morning. You are asleep, cradled in my left arm, and I am learning the art of one-handed typing. Your mother, more tired, yet more happy than I've ever known her, is sound asleep in the room next door. Since you've arrived, days have melted into night and back again.

When you're older we'll tell you that you were born in Britain's last Asian colony in the lunar year of the pig, and that when we brought you home, the staff of our apartment block gathered to wish you well. Your mother and I have wanted you and waited for you, imagined you and dreamed about you, and now that you are here, no dream can do justice to you.

We have called you Daniel Patrick. Your coming has turned me upside down and inside out. So much that seemed essential to me has, in the past few days, taken on a different colour. Like many foreign correspondents I know I have lived a life that on occasion has veered close to the edge: war zones, natural disasters, darkness in all its shapes and forms.

In a world of insecurity and ambition and ego it's easy to be drawn in, to take chances with our lives, to believe that what we do and what people say about it is reason enough to gamble with death. Now, looking at your sleeping face, inches away from me, listening to your occasional sigh and gurgle, I wonder how I could have ever thought glory and prizes and praise were sweeter than life.

And it's also true that I am pained, perhaps haunted is a better word, by the memory, suddenly so vivid now, of each suffering child I have come across on my journeys. Looking at you, the images come flooding back.

Ten-year-old Ani Mikail dying from napalm burns on a hillside in Eritrea, how his voice cried out, growing ever more faint when the wind blew dust onto his wounds.

The two brothers, Domingo and Juste in Menongue, southern Angola. Juste, three years old and blind, dying from malnutrition, being carried on 10-year-old Domingo's back. And Domingo's words to me: 'He was nice before, but now he has the hunger.'

There is one last memory, of Rwanda, and the churchyard of the parish of Nyarabuye, where, in a ransacked classroom, I found a mother and her three young children huddled together where they had been beaten to death. The children had died holding onto their mother, that instinct we all learn from birth and in one way or another cling to until we die.

Daniel, these memories explain some of the fierce protectiveness I feel for you, the occasional moments of blind terror when I imagine anything happening to you. But there is something more, a story from long ago that I will tell you face to face, father to son, when you are older.

It begins 35 years ago in a big city on a January morning with snow on the ground and a woman walking to hospital to have her first baby. She is in her early twenties and the city is still strange to her, bigger and noisier than the easy streets and gentle hills of her distant home. She's walking because there is no money and everything of value has been pawned to pay for the alcohol to which her husband has become addicted.

On the way a taxi driver notices her sitting exhausted and cold in the doorway of a shop and he takes her to hospital for free. Later that day she gives birth to a baby boy and just as you are to me, he is the best thing she has ever seen. Her husband comes that night and weeps with joy when he sees his son. He is truly happy. Hungover, broke, but in his own way happy, for they were both young and in love with each other, and their son.

But the cancer of alcoholism ate away at the man and he lost his family. This was not something he meant to do or wanted to happen, it just was. By the time his son had grown up, the man lived away from his family, on his own in a one-roomed flat, living and dying for the bottle. His son was too far away to hear his last words, his final breath, and all the things they might have wished to say to one another were left unspoken.

Yet, Daniel, when you let out your first powerful cry in the delivery room and I became a father, I thought of your grandfather, and, foolish though it may seem, hoped that in some way he could hear, across the infinity between the living and the dead, your proud statement of arrival. For if he could hear, he would recognize the distinct voice of the family, the sound of hope and new beginnings that you and all your innocence and freshness have brought to the world.

Fergal

A: Letter 1

1 What has happened to create the 'ruined sitting room'?
2 Apart from the date at the top of the first letter, what other clues can you find about when the events in the letter are set?
3 Write down three facts about Fergal Keane's father.
4 What clues are there in the first letter about the age of Fergal Keane at the time of the memory?

A: Letter 2

5 Find a phrase or sentence from the second letter to show that Fergal Keane has lived a hazardous life.
6 Write down three words of your own to show Fergal Keane's feelings for his new son. Beneath each word, write a sentence explaining why you chose it.
7 Say in your own words what you think the writer means by 'these memories explain the fierce protectiveness I feel for you'.

B: Comparisons

8 The writer feels mixed emotions towards his father: write a brief paragraph explaining how he feels.

9 Fergal Keane's family leave their father. Apart from his weaknesses and faults, is there anything to admire about him?

10 Write a paragraph about the way Fergal Keane uses language in both letters. Do you find his written style simple, complex, descriptive, poetic, vivid, precise ...? What tone does each letter have – regretful, emotional, calm, sombre, confused? Support your ideas with specific references from the text.

1 From the two letters together, what picture do you gain of Fergal Keane? Write a brief factual description of him. Imagine that your text will be used in a reference book. Mention:

- his home background
- his character
- his career
- his attitude to his father
- his attitude to his son.

Your opening sentence might read like this: 'Fergal Keane has a powerful memory of an event from his past in 1972 ...' Aim to write five paragraphs.

2 If he were alive, how might Fergal Keane's father respond to reading both letters? What emotions would they create – guilt, anger, disappointment, joy at the birth of a new child? How might he explain his earlier behaviour?
Write a letter of reply entitled, 'Dear Son'. Try to keep the style of your writing similar to Fergal Keane's, and refer to some of the specific memories given in both letters – this time from the father's point of view.

Charles Dickens: Letter to Daniel Maclise, 12 March 1841

Before reading

As well as being the most famous novelist of the nineteenth century, Charles Dickens was also an enthusiastic letter-writer. Here he writes to his friend, the painter Daniel Maclise, to report that his pet raven has died. The letter was sealed with black wax. After Dickens died, the stuffed raven was sold in its glass case for £126.

This might seem an unusual topic for a letter. What do you expect the tone will be like – factual, sad, humorous?

Letter to Daniel Maclise, 12 March 1841

Devonshire Terrace.
Friday Evening
March The Twelfth 1841.

My Dear Maclise,

You will be deeply shocked and grieved to hear that the Raven is no more.

He expired today at a few minutes after Twelve o'Clock at noon. He had been ailing (as I told you t'other night) for a few days, but we anticipated no serious result, conjecturing that a portion of the white paint he swallowed last summer might be lingering about his vitals without having any serious effect upon his constitution. Yesterday afternoon he was taken so much worse that I sent an express for the medical gentleman (Mr Herring) who promptly attended, and administered a powerful dose of castor oil. Under the influence of this medicine, he recovered so far as to be able at 8 o' Clock p.m. to bite Topping. His night was peaceful. This morning at daybreak he appeared better; received (agreeably to the doctor's directions) another dose of castor oil; and partook plentifully of some warm gruel, the flavour of which he appeared to relish. Towards eleven o'Clock he was so much worse that it was found necessary to muffle the stable knocker. At half past, or thereabouts, he was heard talking to himself about the horse and Topping's family, and to add some incoherent expressions which are supposed to have been either a foreboding of his approaching dissolution, or some wishes relative to the disposal of his little property – consisting chiefly of halfpence which he had buried in different parts of the garden. On the clock striking twelve he appeared slightly agitated, but he soon

Word bank
ailing – suffering
Barnaby – Dickens' new novel *Barnaby Rudge* was being published in regular instalments, costing three shillings each
castor oil – yellow oil thought to be good for general health
conjecturing – imagining
constitution – overall health
dissolution – death
equanimity – balanced personality
foreboding – hint
fortitude – strength
gruel – thin soup
incoherent – not making sense
Manna – in the Bible, the food which miraculously dropped from the sky to the Israelites when they were starving in the wilderness
post mortem examination – medical analysis of a dead body
vitals – organs

recovered, walked twice or thrice along the coach-house, stopped to bark, staggered, exclaimed 'Halloa old girl!' (his favourite expression) and died.

He behaved throughout with a decent fortitude, equanimity, and self-possession, which cannot be too much admired. I deeply regret that being in ignorance of his danger I did not attend to receive his last instructions. Something remarkable about his eyes occasioned Topping to run for the doctor at Twelve. When they returned together our friend was gone. It was the medical gentleman who informed me of his decease. He did it with great caution and delicacy, preparing me by the remark that 'a jolly queer start had taken place', but the shock was very great notwithstanding.

I am not wholly free from suspicions of poison – a malicious butcher has been heard to say that he would 'do' for him – his plea was, that he would not be molested in taking orders down the Mews, by any bird that wore a tail – other persons have also been heard to threaten – among others, Charles Knight who has just started a weekly publication, price fourpence; Barnaby being, as you know, Threepence. I have directed a post mortem examination, and the body has been removed to Mr Herring's school of Anatomy for that purpose.

I could wish, if you can take the trouble, that you would inclose this to Forster when you have read it. I cannot discharge the painful task of communication more than once. Were they Ravens who took Manna to somebody in the wilderness? At times I hope they were, and at others I fear they were not, or they would certainly have stolen it by the way. In profound sorrow, I am ever Your bereaved friend. CD.

Kate is as well as can be expected, but terribly low as you may suppose. The children seem rather glad of it. He bit their ankles. But that was play –

Charles Dickens

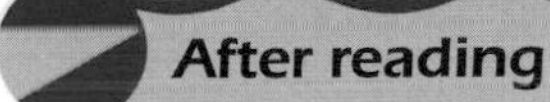

After reading

A

1 When the raven first became ill, what did Dickens think was the cause?
2 What was the first medical treatment the bird received?
3 What was the bird's reaction to the taste of the gruel?
4 Why do you think it was 'necessary to muffle the stable knocker'?

B

5 How does Dickens react to the death of the raven?
6 Why might Charles Knight have had a reason for poisoning the bird?
7 In what ways is the raven presented as if it was a human being?
8 What do you make of the tone of the letter? Is Dickens seriously upset, or does he treat the event as a kind of joke? Write a paragraph explaining your response.

Extended assignments

1 Some people are not sure whether to treat Dickens' letter seriously or not. Rewrite a modern version which is a straightforward, factual account of what happened to the raven.
2 Write Daniel Maclise's response to the letter, expressing your sympathy for Dickens, and requesting details of the raven's funeral. Try to keep the tone as much as possible like Dickens' own.

Holiday Brochure Comparison: Butlin's Breakaways and Shearings Britain

Genre key: Brochures Brochures have many of the elements of leaflets and advertisements, but they have a very specific purpose – to persuade us to choose a holiday from this text. So they use glossy photographs, descriptive writing, and other features to make us wish we were there instead of here.

Before reading

These pages from two holiday brochures both describe holidays in Scotland. But they are aimed at different types of holiday makers.

Skim-read the two texts. What clues can you find about who each one is aimed at?

Word bank
mesmerise – put into a trance

Butlin's Breakaways Brochure

WONDERWEST WORLD

SITUATED ON SCOTLAND'S WEST COAST, WONDERWEST IS OVERFLOWING WITH FUN FILLED FAMILY ENTERTAINMENT

A world packed full of fun and entertainment for all the family – that's the wonder of Wonderwest! No-one need miss out on any of the excitement. Kids will love the wacky fun with the 'Krazzy Krew' while the more mature funseekers will love our adult-only venue. Fabulous all day family shows provide non-stop entertainment while 'Tonix' Leisure Club offers a haven of relaxation.

Wonderwest nights mean big star entertainment, family cabaret and dancing. With so much to cram in, be sure to re-charge your batteries in the variety of food outlets and snack bars. Whether you prefer spectacular night-time entertainment or daytime thrills in a sub-tropical waterworld with plunge pools and fabulous flume rides, Wonderwest provides the best of both worlds.

INCLUDED IN THE PRICE OF YOUR BREAKAWAY!

- ★ Sub-Tropical Waterworld 'Wondersplash'
- ★ Limited range of Funfair & Junior Funfair Rides
- ★ Kids' Entertainment
- ★ Family & Adult Only Showbars

- ★ Live Cabaret & Entertainment
- ★ Leisure & Sports Activities
- ★ Dancing
- ★ Disco... and more

CENTRAL HIGHLANDS

The combination of water and mountains is ever present in this corner of Scotland, where there's a raw kind of magic in the air. The Isle of Bute presents an ever-changing kaleidoscope of colour and beauty and is the setting for Rothesay, lying on a sweeping bay with panoramic views of hills and sea. Dunoon, nestling on the shores of the Firth of Clyde and backed by the bens, glens and lochs of the splendid Cowal Peninsula, offers a real taste of the Highlands and a wealth of interesting sightseeing opportunities; as does Tarbet, where there's a terrific panorama of rippling Loch Lomond, famed for its tranquil beauty, and the heather-clad slopes of mighty Ben Lomond, which will surely mesmerise.

Tarbet Hotel, Tarbet, Loch Lomond

The Tarbet, some two hundred years old, is built in true Scottish baronial style, and although its facilities have been upgraded as time has gone by, the hotel's traditional character has been retained. Set across the road from the shores of beautiful Loch Lomond, it has an enviable view, over the water, to the heather-clad slopes of Ben Lomond.

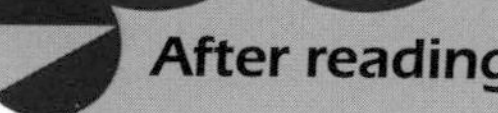

After reading

A

1 What does the Butlin's holiday have for children?
2 What does it offer for adults?
3 What is the main feature on offer in the Shearings brochure?
4 Choose a sentence from each brochure which you think best sums up the kind of holiday it is offering.

B

5 Look at this list of adjectives from each brochure. Write a sentence saying what they show about the different audiences each is aimed at:

Butlin's	Shearings
packed	raw
wacky	ever-changing
non-stop	sweeping
spectacular	panoramic
sub-tropical	interesting
fabulous	tranquil
	heather-clad

6 Which brochure gives more information? Explain your answer.
7 Which holiday would you prefer? Write a paragraph explaining why.

Extended assignments

1 Look again at the language style of either brochure. Imagine your school is going to be used as a holiday centre with a campsite to make money in the summer vacations. Try to write a page from a brochure advertising it, using the style of one of the brochures here.
2 Imagine that Butlin's want to attract older people and Shearings want to attract younger ones. Redesign and rewrite one of the brochures to try to make it appeal to the different audience. Then write a paragraph explaining your approach and how well you think it has worked.

Peggy Noonan: The Future Doesn't Belong to the Fainthearted

Genre key: Speeches Even in a hi-tech media age, speeches continue to matter. Politicians, teachers, lawyers, judges, and many others use them almost daily. The best speeches are designed to persuade us to think or do something.

Before reading

On 28 January, 1986, the US space shuttle *Challenger* blasted off from Cape Canaveral, only to explode shortly after take-off. The world watched on television sets and responded with horror and shock. One member of the crew was a schoolteacher – the first civilian in space. Every American school had followed her progress with pride. Space travel could never be the same again, its risks terrifyingly on show. That night US President Ronald Reagan was due to address the American people. His speech-writer, Peggy Noonan, rewrote his words, trying to sum up the mood of people across the world.

The Future Doesn't Belong to the Fainthearted

Word bank
pioneers – explorers of a new land
Sir Francis Drake – English navigator (1540–96); the first Englishman to sail around the world (1577–80)
surly – rude, sulky

Nineteen years ago, almost to the day, we lost three astronauts in a terrible accident on the ground. But we've never lost an astronaut in flight; we've never had a tragedy like this. And perhaps we've forgotten the courage it took for the crew of the shuttle; but they, the *Challenger* Seven, were aware of the dangers, but overcame them and did their jobs brilliantly. We mourn seven heroes: Michael Smith, Dick Scobee, Judith Resnick, Ronald McNair, Ellison Onizuka, Gregory Jarvis, and Christa McAuliffe. We mourn their loss as a nation together.

For the families of the seven, we cannot bear, as you do, the full impact of this tragedy. But we feel the loss, and we're thinking about you so very much. Your loved ones were daring and brave, and they had that special grace, that special spirit that says, 'Give me a challenge and I'll meet it with joy.' They had a hunger to explore the universe and discover its truths. They wished to serve, and they did. They served all of us.

We've grown used to wonders in this century. It's hard to dazzle us. But for twenty-five years the United States space programme has been doing just that. We've grown used to the idea of space, and perhaps we forget that we've only just begun. We're still pioneers. They, the members of the *Challenger* crew, were pioneers.

And I want to say something to the schoolchildren of America who were watching the live coverage of the shuttle's take-off. I know it is hard to understand, but sometimes painful things like this happen. It's all part of the process of exploration and discovery. It's all part of taking a chance and expanding man's horizons. The future doesn't belong to the fainthearted; it belongs to the brave. The *Challenger* crew was pulling us into the future, and we'll continue to follow them...

There's a coincidence today. On this day 390 years ago, the great explorer Sir Francis Drake died aboard ship off the coast of Panama. In his lifetime the great frontiers were the oceans, and a historian later said, 'He lived by the sea, died on it, and was buried in it.' Well, today we can say of the *Challenger* crew: their dedication was, like Drake's, complete.

The crew of the space shuttle *Challenger* honoured us by the manner in which they lived their lives. We will never forget them, nor the last time we saw them, this morning, as they prepared for this journey and waved goodbye and 'slipped the surly bonds of earth' to 'touch the face of God'.

Peggy Noonan

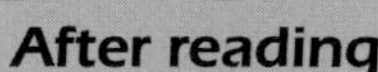

After reading

A

1. Look at the first paragraph again. Pick out a word or phrase which shows that the writer admires the astronauts.
2. Why do you think she names the crew one by one?
3. Look at paragraph 2. How does Peggy Noonan show sympathy for the families of the astronauts?
4. Why do you think in paragraph 3 she describes the crew as 'pioneers'?

5 Near the end of the speech, Peggy Noonan refers to Sir Francis Drake. In a sentence, describe the point she makes.

B

6 In her speech, Peggy Noonan uses the word 'we' a lot, rather than 'I'. Why do you think this is?
7 Pick out three words or phrases which you think are particularly powerful and write a sentence about each one describing why you think it works so well.
8 How does the writer use repetition of words and phrases to create a powerful effect? Give some examples to support your ideas.
9 Read the comment of this reader:
'It's a clever speech, but it's very sickly. It has nothing specific to say, just lots of vague, emotional words. It sounds good but means little.'
Write a paragraph saying how far you agree or disagree with this point of view.

1 Based on your answers to the questions above, write a commentary on this speech. Comment on: the ideas; the words; the use of repetition; the way the astronauts are described; the reference to the families; the reference to the viewers. How successful do you find the speech overall?
2 Choose a topic you feel strongly about and write a two-minute speech to persuade the audience to agree with you. Try to: use emotional words; use repetition; make the audience feel involved by saying 'we' and 'us'; give specific examples, facts, and statistics to convince your audience to believe you; use questions to make the audience more involved.

Chief Seattle: Your God is not Our God

Before reading

Chief Seattle was Chief of the native American tribe of Suquamish. As a boy he saw the first explorers arriving from Britain, and he later encouraged his people to live with the new settlers rather than to fight against them. But as more white settlers arrived, so relationships broke down. In 1855 a treaty was drawn up to remove all native Americans to reservations – special areas where they could live, whilst all of their previous land was retained by the settlers. Seattle agreed, and signed the treaty, and this is part of his acceptance speech. It was originally delivered in Seattle's native language, Salish.

The American west-coast city of Seattle was named in memory of this most famous Indian chief.

How do you think the Chief will sound in handing over the land of his people to new settlers – angry, calm, disappointed, worried about the future ...?

Your God is not Our God

Word bank
disfigured – ruined
fastnesses – strongholds, safe places
firmament – heavens
forsaken – abandoned
impulsive – acting hastily
our good father at Washington – Isaac Stevens, first governor of Washington and supervisor of Indian affairs
partial – biased; one-sided
Sachems – native chiefs or elders

The Great – and I presume – good White Chief sends us word that he wants to buy our lands but is willing to allow us to reserve enough to live on comfortably. This indeed appears generous, for the Red Man no longer has rights that he need respect, and the offer may be wise, also, for we are no longer in need of a great country.

There was a time when our people covered the whole land as the waves of a wind-ruffled sea covers its shell-paved floor, but that time has long since passed away with the greatness of tribes now almost forgotten. I will not dwell on nor mourn over our untimely decay, nor reproach my paleface brothers with hastening it, for we, too, may have been somewhat to blame.

Youth is impulsive. When our young men grow angry at some real or imaginary wrong, and disfigure their faces with black paint, their hearts are also disfigured and turn black, and then they are often cruel and relentless and know no bounds, and our old men are unable to restrain them.

Thus it has ever been. Thus it was when the white man first began to push our forefathers westward. But let us hope that the hostilities between the Red Man and his paleface brother may never return. We would have everything to lose and nothing to gain.

It is true that revenge by young braves is considered gain, even at the cost of their own lives, but old men who stay at home in times of war, and mothers who have sons to lose, know better.

Our good father in Washington – for I presume he is now our father as well as yours, since King George has moved his boundaries farther north – our great and good father, I say, sends us word that if we do as he desires he will protect us.

His brave warriors will be to us a bristling wall of strength, and his great ships of war will fill our harbors so that our ancient enemies far to the northward – the Sinsiams, Hydas and Tsimpsians – will no longer frighten our women and old men. Then will he be our father and we his children.

But can that ever be? Your God is not our God! Your God loves your people and hates mine! He folds His strong arms lovingly around the white man and leads him as a father leads his infant son – but He has forsaken His red children, if they are really His. Our God, the Great Spirit, seems, also, to have forsaken us. Your God makes your people wax strong every day – soon they will fill all the land.

My people are ebbing away like a fast-receding tide that will never flow again. The white man's God cannot love His red children or He would protect them. We seem to be orphans who can look nowhere for help.

How, then, can we become brothers? How can your God become our God and renew our prosperity and awaken in us dreams of returning greatness?

Your God seems to us to be partial. He came to the white man. We never saw Him, never heard His voice. He gave the white man laws, but had no word for His red children whose teeming millions once filled this vast continent as the stars fill the firmament.

No. We are two distinct races, and must ever remain so, with separate origins and separate destinies. There is little in common between us.

To us the ashes of our ancestors are sacred and their final resting place is hallowed ground, while you wander far from the graves of your ancestors and, seemingly, without regret.

Your religion was written on tablets of stone by the iron finger of an angry God, lest you might forget it. The Red Man could never comprehend nor remember it.

Our religion is the traditions of our ancestors – the dreams of our old men, given to them in the solemn hours of night by the Great Spirit, and the visions of our Sachems, and is written in the hearts of our people.

Your dead cease to love you and the land of their nativity as soon as they pass the portals of the tomb – they wander far away beyond the stars, are soon forgotten and never return.

Our dead never forget this beautiful world that gave them being. They still love its winding rivers, its great mountains and its

sequestered vales, and they ever yearn in tenderest affection over the lonely-hearted living, and often return to visit, guide and comfort them.

Day and night cannot dwell together. The Red Man has ever fled the approach of the white man, as the changing mist on the mountain side flees before the blazing sun.

Every part of this country is sacred to my people. Every hillside, every valley, every plain and grove has been hallowed by some fond memory or some sad experience of my tribe. Even the rocks, which seem to lie dumb as they swelter in the sun along the silent sea shore in solemn grandeur, thrill with memories of past events connected with the lives of my people.

The very dust under your feet responds more lovingly to our footsteps than to yours, because it is the ashes of our ancestors, and our bare feet are conscious of the sympathetic touch, for the soil is rich with the life of our kindred.

The noble braves, fond mothers, glad, happy-hearted maidens, and even the little children, who lived and rejoiced here for a brief season, and whose very names are now forgotten, still love these sombre solitudes and their deep fastnesses which, at eventide, grow shadowy with the presence of dusky spirits.

And when the last Red Man shall have perished from the earth and his memory among the white men shall have become a myth, these shores will swarm with the invisible dead of my tribe; and when your children's children shall think of themselves alone in the fields, the store, the shop, upon the highway, or in the silence of the pathless woods, they will not be alone. In all the earth there is no place dedicated to solitude.

At night, when the streets of your cities and villages will be silent and you think them deserted, they will throng with the returning hosts that once filled and still love this beautiful land.

The white man will never be alone. Let him be just and deal kindly with my people, for the dead are not powerless.

Dead – did I say? There is no death. Only a change of worlds!

Chief Seattle

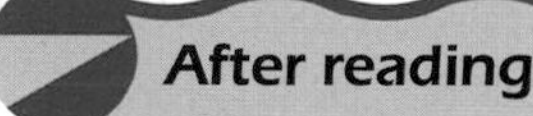

A

1 Chief Seattle is responding to the offer of money to buy native American lands. Does he think it is a fair offer?

2 Chief Seattle lists the differences between his own people and the white settlers. What are some of these differences? Fill in a table like this one, based on what he says in his speech (an example is done for you). Aim to find three differences between the two peoples.

Native Americans	**White Settlers**
Not loved by God	Loved by God

3 Which of these words do you think best sums up Chief Seattle's feelings? Write down the word and then a sentence or paragraph explaining your choice:

sad disappointed angry contented tired bitter

B

4 Look again at the last three short paragraphs of Chief Seattle's speech. Say in your own words what you think he means.

5 How can you tell that this is a speech rather than, say, a diary or an autobiography? Write a paragraph about its persuasive features. You might mention:

- who the text seems to be addressed to
- repetition of important or emotional words
- the rhythm of the words and phrases within sentences
- use of questions.

1 Chief Seattle's speech is full of powerful repetitions and pictures. Try reducing it to around 150 words, keeping the basic message the same. Use a mixture of your own words and those of the Chief.

Then write a paragraph explaining:

- what you decided to cut and what to keep
- what problems you encountered
- what has been gained and lost in the new version.

2 Imagine you were making the speech into a television party political broadcast – a three-minute programme aimed at persuading viewers to accept this message. Imagine you have sixteen different frames to use, and in each one there will be an image and some spoken words. This will be easiest to do if you first look at the key ideas in the speech – perhaps summarizing them, as suggested in Activity 1.

Then, for each frame, say what your image would be (close-up of the Chief speaking, picture of Indian people, image of sea, river, trees, etc.). Underneath, write the words that would be spoken over the top.

Then write a paragraph explaining your choice of images and text, and highlighting the difficulties you encountered.

Advertisements Comparison: Help the Aged and RSPCA

Genre key: Advertisements

We are surrounded by advertising. Whether it is in newspapers, on billboards, on television or on radio, it is all designed to persuade us that a certain product is attractive. The basic message of much advertising is, 'this product will make you feel or look better'. Advertisements to persuade us to support certain organizations have to try other techniques.

Before reading

Word bank
faeces – body waste

The two advertisements on pages 158 and 159 have an important purpose. They want us to do more than read them. They want us then to do something – to help animals and to help elderly people. (The 'Help the Aged' advertisment was published in 1987, so the statistics are no longer accurate – but the message is still relevant.)

Which advertisements in newspapers or magazines have stuck in your memory?

After reading

A

1. Who do you think the advertisements are aimed at?
2. How do they use presentation and language to persuade us to help?
3. How do they try to get an emotional response from us?
4. Which do you think works best? Say why.

Extended assignments

1. Choose a cause you feel strongly about and design an advertisement to make people stop and think. Don't worry too much about pictures – just label what the images would be rather than spend a long time drawing them. Then write a paragraph describing the techniques you used.
2. Choose one or two print advertisements that you think are good; chose one or two which you consider poor. Write about them all, saying what you admire and dislike in them, and paying close attention to their layout and language.

TEST YOUR POWERS OF INDIFFERENCE

1. **How many households in the United Kingdom are an old person living alone?**
   ☐ 1 in 30 ☐ 1 in 13 ☐ 1 in 10 ☐ 1 in 7
2. **How many old people have no living relatives?**
   ☐ 50,000 ☐ 100,000 ☐ 300,000 ☐ 500,000
3. **How many old people have no regular visitors?**
   ☐ 200,000 ☐ 450,000 ☐ 750,000 ☐ 1,000,000
4. **How many old people cannot get in and out of bed unaided?**
   ☐ 20,000 ☐ 34,000 ☐ 70,000 ☐ 189,000 ☐ 500,000
5. **How many old people died in their homes from the cold in 1985?**
   ☐ 200 ☐ 571 ☐ 1,000 ☐ 10,512 ☐ 100,000
6. **Britain has 1.1 million dwellings statutorily defined as unfit for human habitation. How many are inhabited by old people?**
   ☐ 50,000 ☐ 150,000 ☐ 250,000 ☐ 350,000 ☐ 500,000
7. **How old was:**
   a) Winston Churchill when he first became Prime Minister?
   b) Michelangelo when he started work on St. Peter's, Rome?
8. **How many centenarians received congratulatory telegrams from the Queen a) in 1965? b) in 1985?**
9. **How many old people depend upon Supplementary Benefit?**
   ☐ ½ million ☐ 1 million ☐ 2 million ☐ 3 million ☐ 4 million ☐ 5 million
10. **What are we doing about it?**

TEST YOUR POWERS OF COMMITMENT.

1. **One household in seven in the UK is an old person living alone.**

   Help the Aged funds day centres throughout the country. For many old people, day centres are their only chance of companionship.
2. **Nearly half a million old people have no living relatives.**

   Help the Aged is aiming to place one minibus every week with voluntary groups. For no less than 20,000 old people who already use this service every week, it is a vital link with the community.
3. **One million old people have no regular visitors.**

   Help the Aged's Lifeline Appeal has already placed nearly 1,000 emergency alarm systems in the homes of old people who are vulnerable and at risk.
4. **189,000 old people cannot get in and out of bed unaided. 695,000 can't cope with stairs. 757,000 can't bath or shower without help. 1,056,000 can't walk unassisted.**

   Help the Aged is funding day hospitals where old people can recover their independence and confidence, after illness or injury.
5. **Last year, 571 old people died in their homes from hypothermia. This year, the figure will be much higher.**

   Besides campaigning for better heating subsidies and better pensions, the day centres we support provide warmth and a hot meal, for some old people their only regular hot meal.
6. **500,000 dwellings – nearly half of our most appalling housing – is inhabited by old people; who are least able to cope.**

   Help the Aged is campaigning for better housing provision for old people, both in the public and private sectors, because old people aren't "them", they're one in five of us.
7. **Winston Churchill was 65 when he became Prime Minister. Michelangelo was 71 when he started work on St. Peter's, Rome.**

   A reminder that being 60+ can be the beginning, not the end of a lifetime's achievements.
8. **In 1965, 448 centenarians received a congratulatory telegram from the Queen. In 1985, the figure was 1,819.**

   Between 1981 and 2001, the number of people aged over 75 will increase from 3.1 million to 4.1 million. More and more of us are going to live to be old. Yet what is in store for us if we let things ride?
9. **Nearly two million old people depend upon supplementary benefit.**

   Put another way, that's one in five pensioners.
10. These facts paint a grim picture of what it can mean to be old in Britain today. Help the Aged is dedicated to improving this situation by campaigning for better pensions and heating allowances. Funding Day Centres, Day Hospitals and Hospices. Providing emergency alarm systems and minibuses. To find out more about our work, or if you would like to make a donation, please write to:
    John Mayo OBE,
    Director-General,
    Help the Aged, Freepost,
    St. James's Walk,
    London EC1B 1BD.

Help the Aged
25TH ANNIVERSARY APPEAL
Patron: The Princess of Wales

Before they're roasted in garlic and rosemary they're soaked in urine and excrement.

The trucks that carry livestock across Europe hold up to 800 sheep at a time.

The journeys can last over twenty-four hours, but the animals' bladders cannot. They begin to urinate and excrete inside the lorry.

One sheep produces around a litre of urine and 700 grammes of faeces a day.

And so do the other 799.

Since they are trapped in such a confined space their fleeces quickly become coated in droppings.

For the rest of the trip they're wet, cold and some even suffer skin burns.

Eventually the urinating stops, but only because the animals are given no water in transit.

The size of Continental trucks means that unfamiliar flocks are often mixed together (an unsettling experience for any animal).

In the crush the weaker sheep lose their footing, fall to the floor and are trampled by the others.

Some die.

And all this happens so European meat traders can squeeze a little more profit from their livestock.

The sheep could be slaughtered close to their farms, refrigerated and then transported (a method favoured by many farmers).

But offal and hides fetch a slightly higher price abroad and freshly killed meat is also at a premium, so the practice continues.

At least until the law is changed.

EC agriculture ministers are about to meet to discuss livestock transportation regulations.

The RSPCA want to see an eight hour limit on the transportation of live animals for slaughter enforced immediately across the European Community.

Britain's representative at the negotiations is Gillian Shephard and there's still time to let her know your views on the crucial issue of maximum journey time.

Which is why we need your help.

Please phone the number below for a free RSPCA information pack and to find out what further action you can take.

Perhaps we can then persuade Mrs Shephard to look after our sheep.

RSPCA

ACKNOWLEDGEMENTS

The author and publisher are grateful for permission to reprint the following copyright material:

Section 1 Fiction

James Berry: extract from 'The Banana Tree' from *A Thief in the Village* (Hamish Hamilton Children's Books, 1987), Copyright © James Berry, 1987, reprinted by permission of Penguin Books Ltd and The Peters Fraser & Dunlop Group Ltd. **Ray Bradbury**: extract from 'The House Began to Die' from *There Will Come Soft Rains* by Ray Bradbury reprinted by permision of Abner Stein. **Berlie Doherty**: extract from 'Bella's Den' first published in Michael Morpurgo (ed): *Muck and Magic* (Heinemann/Mammoth, 1995), reprinted by permission of David Higham Associates. **Sir Arthur Conan Doyle**: extract from 'The Engineer's Thumb' from *The Adventures of Sherlock Holmes*, Copyright © Sheldon Reynolds, 1996, reproduced by kind permission of Jonathan Clowes Ltd., London, on behalf of Sheldon Reynolds. **Eleanor Farjeon**: extract from 'Grendel The Monster' in *Mighty Men* (Basil Blackwell, 1925), reprinted by permission of David Higham Associates. **Rosa Guy**: 'She' from Donald D Gallo (ed): *Sixteen* (Fontana Lions, 1987), reprinted by permission of HarperCollins Publishers Ltd. **Jan Mark**: extract from 'Nule' in *Nothing to be Afraid Of* (Kestrel Books, 1980), Copyright © Jan Mark, 1980, reprinted by permission of Penguin Books Ltd. **Ruth Rendell**: 'The Clinging Woman' from *The Fallen Curtain and Other Stories* by Ruth Rendell (Hutchinson, 1976), reprinted by permission of Random House UK Ltd on behalf of the author. **H G Wells**: extract from *War of the Worlds* reprinted by permission of A P Watt Ltd on behalf of The Literary Executors of the Estate of H G Wells. **Robert Westall**: 'Rosalie' from *Ghosts and Journeys* (Macmillan Children's Books), Copyright © Robert Westall 1988, reprinted by permission of the Laura Cecil Literary Agency on behalf of the Estate of Robert Westall.

Section 2 Drama

Dawn French and Jennifer Saunders: 'The Health Expert', reproduced by permission of Peters Fraser & Dunlop Artists on behalf of the authors. **Joyce Grenfell**: 'Going Home Time' from *George ... Don't Do That...* (Macmillan, 1977), Copyright © Joyce Grenfell 1977, 1978, reprinted by permission of Richard Scott Simon Ltd. **Louis Phillips**: extract from one-act play 'Carwash', first published in *Crazy Quilt*, reprinted by permission of the author. **Bernard Shaw**: extract from *Pygmalion*, reprinted by permission of The Society of Authors on behalf of the Bernard Shaw Estate. **Michael Wilcox**: opening of playscript for 'Last Bus to Woodstock', Copyright © Carlton Television, reprinted by permission of Carlton Television and The International Copyright Bureau Ltd on behalf of the author.

Section 3 Poetry

Vicki Feaver: 'Slow Reader', first published in the *Times Literary Supplement*, reprinted by permission of the author. **Thom Gunn**: 'Baby Song' from *Jack Straw's Castle*, reprinted by permission of the publishers, Faber & Faber Ltd. **Seamus Heaney**: extract from 'A Sofa in the Forties' from *The Spirit Level*, and extract from 'Mossbawn' in *Preoccupations: Selected Prose 1968-1978*, both reprinted by permission of the publishers, Faber & Faber Ltd. **Rudyard Kipling**: 'The Way Through the Woods' from *A Choice of Kipling's Verse* edited by T S Eliot (Faber 1963), reprinted by permission of A P Watt Ltd on behalf of The National Trust. **Philip Larkin**: 'The North Ship' from *Collected Poems*, reprinted by permission of the publishers, Faber & Faber Ltd. **Louis MacNeice**: 'Prayer Before Birth' from *Collected Poems* (Faber), reprinted by permission of David Higham Associates. **Jack Mapanje**: 'The Sweet Brew at Chitakale' from *Of Chameleons and Gods* (Heinemann Educational Books), Copyright © Jack Mapanje 1981, reprinted by permission of Heinemann Publishers Oxford. **Carole Satyamurti**: 'Day Trip' from *Broken Moon* by Carole Satyamurti (OUP, 1987), reprinted by permission of Oxford University Press. **Anne Stevenson**: 'The Fish Are All Sick' from *The Collected Poems 1955-1995* (OUP, 1996), reprinted by permission of Oxford University Press. **Derek Walcott**: 'Dark August' from *Sea Grapes* (Jonathan Cape), reprinted by permission of Random House UK Ltd on behalf of the author. **Judith Wright**: 'Rainforest' from *A Human Pattern: Selected Poems* (ETT Imprint, Watsons Bay 1996), reprinted by permission of the publishers.

Section 4 Non-Fiction

Mulk Raj Anand: extract from *Seven Summers: The Story of an Indian Childhood* (Century Hutchinson 1951), reprinted by permission of the author. **Butlin's** Breakaways brochure, Sept 96–April 97, extract about Wonderwest World, reproduced by permission of ParkWorld Holidays Ltd. **Charles Dickens**: extract from 1841 letter from *The Pilgrim Edition of the Letters of Charles Dickens*, vol. 2 edited by Madeline House and Graham Storey (OUP, 1969), reprinted by permission of Oxford University Press. **Nicholas Fisk**: extract from *Pig Ignorant* (Walker Books, 1992), Copyright © 1992 Nicholas Fisk. Permission granted by the publisher Walker Books Ltd. **Jonathan Freedland**: article from *The Guardian*, Copyright © The Guardian 1996, reprinted by permission of the publishers. **Help the Aged**: advertisement, reprinted with permission. **Fergal Keane**: letters first published in *The Independent*, Copyright © Fergal Keane 1996, reproduced by permission of the author c/o Rogers, Coleridge & White, 20 Powis Mews, London W11 1JN. **Blake Morrison**: extract from *And When Did You Last See Your Father?* (Granta/Penguin, 1993), Copyright © 1993 by Blake Morrison, reprinted by permission of Penguin Books Ltd. **Peggy Noonan**: extract from speech written for Ronald Reagan from *What I Saw at the Revolution*, Copyright © 1989 by Peggy Noonan, reprinted by permission of International Creative Management, Inc. **Frances Partridge**: extract from *Julia: A Portrait by Herself and Frances Partridge* (first published by Victor Gollancz, 1983), Copyright © the Estate of Julia Strachey, 1983, reproduced by permission of Frances Partridge c/o Rogers, Coleridge and White Ltd., 20 Powis Mews, London W11 1JN. **RSPCA**: advertisement, reproduced by permission. **Shearings Holidays Limited**: extracts from *British Breaks* brochure, Winter 1996/97. **Nicole Veash**: article from *The Yorkshire Evening Press*, reprinted by permission of the publishers.

Although every effort has been made to trace and contact copyright holders before publication, we have not been successful in a few cases. If notified the publisher will be pleased to rectify any errors or omissions at the earliest opportunity.

We would also like to thank the following for permission to reproduce photographs:

p 26 illustration from *Beowulf* by Charles Keeping (Oxford University Press 1982) reproduced by kind permission of Mrs Renate Keeping; p 29 (detail) William Bell Scott (1811–90) 'The Lamentation of King Arthur', The Bridgeman Art Library / Whitford & Hughes, London; pp 60, 61 by permission of Peters Fraser & Dunlop and BBC Television; pp 69, 70 by permission of Carlton UK Television; pp 78, 80 Donald Cooper / Photostage; p 87 Oxford Scientific Films / Martyn Chillmaid; p 91 Oxford Scientific Films / Animals Animals / Zig Leszczynski; p 92 Science Photo Library / BSIP, Delacourt; p 108–109 Oxford Scientific Films / Derek Bromhall; p 113 (main picture) Science Photo Library / A. Gragera, Latin Stock; p 113 (top right) Chris Honeywell; p 115 Sally & Richard Greenhill; p 127 Peter Newark's Historical Pictures; p 132 Oxford Scientific Films / Survival Anglia / Alan Root; p 146 by permission of ParkWorld Holidays; p 147 Oxford Scientific Films / G. A. Maclean; p 149 Science Photo Library / NASA; p 154 Peter Newark's American Pictures.

The illustrations are by:

Peter Allsop pp 48, 49; David Axtell pp 39, 61, 62, 100, 167, 168; John Dunne pp 21, 23, 107; Ian Foulis & Assoc. p 34; Rosamund Fowler pp 115, 116, 122, 123; Robert Goldsmith pp 113, 125, 140; Clive Goodyer pp 36, 83, 86; Paul Hunt pp 11, 42; Gillian Hunt c/o Specs Art pp 144, 175, 176, 180; Ivan Lapper pp 17, 58; Jackie McQuade pp 51, 54, 118; Alan Marks pp 70, 71, 120; Tony Morris c/o L Rogers Assoc. pp 21, 23, 107.

Cover and title page: 'Progress, 1973' by Lucien Mathelin, reproduced by permission of The Bridgeman Art Library.